# LOVE &
# RESPECT
### *in the*
# family

# LOVE & RESPECT

## *in the* family

The Respect Parents Desire;
The Love Children Need

## DR. EMERSON EGGERICHS

W PUBLISHING GROUP

AN IMPRINT OF THOMAS NELSON

Published in Nashville, Tennessee, by W Publishing Group. W Publishing is a registered trademark of Thomas Nelson.

Author is represented by the literary agency of Alive Communications, Inc., 7680 Goddard Street, Suite 200, Colorado Springs, CO 80920, www.alivecommunications.com.

Thomas Nelson titles may be purchased in bulk for educational, business, fund-raising, or sales promotional use. For information, please e-mail SpecialMarkets@ ThomasNelson.com.

Unless otherwise indicated, Scripture quotations are taken from the New American Standard Bible®. © The Lockman Foundation 1960, 1962, 1963, 1968, 1971, 1972, 1973, 1975, 1977, 1995. Used by permission.

Other Scripture references are taken from the following sources: Contemporary English Version (CEV). © 1991 by the American Bible Society. Used by permission. English Standard Version (ESV). © 2001 by Crossway Bibles, a division of Good News Publishers. The English Translation of the Septuagint by Sir Lancelot Charles Lee Brenton (1807–1862) (BRENTON), originally published in 1851. Good News Translation (GNT). © 1976, 1992 by the American Bible Society. Used by permission. All rights reserved. God's Word Translation (GW). © 1995 by God's Word to the Nations. Used by permission of Baker Publishing Group. King James Version of the Bible (KJV). Public domain. *The Message* (M SG) by Eugene H. Peterson. © 1993, 1994, 1995, 1996, 2000. Used by permission of NavPress Publishing Group. All rights reserved. New King James Version® (NKJV). © 1982 by Thomas Nelson, Inc. Used by permission. All rights reserved. New International Reader's Version® (NIRV). © 1996, 1998 by Biblica, Inc.™ Used by permission of Zondervan. All rights reserved worldwide. Holy Bible, New International Version®, NIV® (NIV). © 1973, 1978, 1984, 2011 by Biblica, Inc.™ Used by permission of Zondervan. All rights reserved worldwide. Holy Bible, New Living Translation (NLT). © 1996. Used by permission of Tyndale House Publishers, Inc., Wheaton, Illinois 60189. All rights reserved.

ISBN 978-0-8499-2205-3 (IE)

**Library of Congress Cataloging-in-Publication Data.**

Eggerichs, Emerson.
  Love & respect in the family : the respect parents desire; the love children need / Emerson Eggerichs.
     pages cm
  Includes bibliographical references.
  ISBN 978-0-8499-4820-6 (hardcover)
1. Parent and child—Religious aspects—Christianity. 2. Parenting—Religious aspects—Christianity. 3. Families—Religious aspects—Christianity. I. Title. II. Title: Love and respect in the family.
  BV4529.E34 2013
  248.4—dc23

                    2013025602

*Printed in the United States of America*

13 14 15 16 17 RRD 5 4 3 2 1

*With love and respect, I dedicate this book to my family.*

*To Sarah: for being an exceedingly better mother than I was a father. As the Bible states, "Her children praise her, and with great pride her husband says, 'There are many good women, but you are the best!'" (Proverbs 31:28–29 CEV).*

*To Jonathan, David, and Joy: You have grown into mature, caring, responsible adults who greatly honor us as your parents. I know you can recall many times you needed to forgive us for failing to meet your needs for love and respect, but we all kept getting back up and growing together. Thank you, Eggerichs kids! Mom and I feel about you just as Psalm 127:3 proclaims, "Children are a blessing and a gift from the LORD" (CEV).*

# CONTENTS

# Contents

# ACKNOWLEDGMENTS

I thank my godly, wise wife, Sarah, for her prayers, counsel, and transparency. Without her immeasurable contribution, I could not have written this book. Truly, she gave birth to this book, laboring with these kids in ways I cannot imagine. Thank you, honey!

I thank Jonathan, David, and Joy for reading each chapter as I wrote it and giving me honest feedback. Without them, I would not and could not have written this book.

I thank Fritz Ridenour for working with me for two years on this book. He has endured my plethora of information, thirty-five years of notes! I am eternally grateful to him for helping me, but more importantly for being my friend. Let me add, that as an octogenarian he has created in me a desire to be as strong, wise, and witty as he is when I am passing into my eighties. He is nothing short of remarkable.

I thank Joanne Tims, Sarah's BFF since college days, for being a third set of eyes at the last hour. Her edits blessed Fritz and me more than she will ever know. She was truly a gift to us.

I thank my sweet daughter-in-law, Sarah, for her reading of the manuscript and helping during the final edits. She caught things none of us saw!

I thank the many people who have written me over the years to share how they applied love and respect in their families.

Many times I was moved to tears. I have changed many names and shifted some details to protect the innocent, but all the testimonies in this book are true indeed.

I thank Rick Christian with Alive Communications and those at Thomas Nelson under Matt Baugher's leadership for their vision to take *Love & Respect in the Family* to the world.

I thank the Love & Respect staff and board for their prayers and support and affirmation that this book needed writing in order to serve parents and children.

I thank my mom and dad, who came to Christ my freshman year in college. At that point our family began to change. We forgave the past, loved and respected each other in the present, and looked forward to eternal life with Christ. Mom and Dad are now in a place Jesus called Paradise. I thank the Lord for my dear sister, Ann, who prays faithfully for me in their absence. They are forever experiencing His perfect love and glory.

I thank our loving Lord for His revelation about children honoring their parents and parents loving their children and for His illumination on how to parent His way—*no matter what.*

# A Personal Word About and from the Eggerichs Children

I waited to write this book until my children were grown. All three are now in their thirties. It is time, but first I would like to say something about them and have you hear from them.

## About Them . . .

Having served as a clinical psychologist and lieutenant in the U.S. Navy for four years, Jonathan launched Love and Respect Counseling P.C. in Grand Rapids, Michigan. He desires to help people who struggle with major life issues, such as the challenges from military deployment, marriage conflicts, or everyday questions of the soul. He pursued clinical psychology as a profession because he wanted to make a difference in people's lives.

David has considerable skills in video production, and owns his own film company, Motivity Pictures. He has helped us numerous times in capturing on video the Love & Respect message. Although he confesses he struggled more than his siblings did with the way we parented, he also claims he is my biggest fan. Recently he came to me with a request to talk to a group of his married friends about how to be good parents. He felt they were missing the mark and told me, "Dad, I know if you could sit down with them and teach them, they'd listen to you. They need to hear what you have to say."

Working for Love and Respect Ministries, Joy has her own national ministry among her generation, speaking to the vital importance of wisdom in relationships. Her website, loveand respectNOW.com, provides many nuggets of her wisdom. Recently, we did a video series together called the Illumination Project. As father and daughter we share insights with young adults, ages eighteen to thirty-five, on how to do love and respect in relationships. We are praying that our transparency—sharing our warts and all—will help others.

## From Them . . .

**Jonathan:** As a clinical psychologist, I often hear from clients what poor parenting, no parenting, or even evil parenting feels like. It leaves me very sad and angry. On the other hand, I also hear clients express a hope and desire to be something different, to change a legacy. They want knowledge, tools, and wisdom. That is one reason why I supported my father in writing this book. Others are more personal.

When I think of what good parents look like, I think of my parents. Am I biased? Yes. But they created that positive bias based on their love and efforts. Were they perfect? No, and I know there were times growing up when I thought they were far from it. However, I'm sure my bias will age and mature like a very expensive wine as the years roll on and my wife and I grow our young family, seeking sips of their wisdom.

Finally, my father expressed doubt about writing this book

based on his perceived failures. My response to that? "Stop it; cut it out. You guys were good enough and well beyond that. You desired to follow Christ and do what seemed best. I know the book will affect others; write it." I wholeheartedly endorse this book, based on my parents' effort and dedication to us as children and the impact I believe it will have on others. Even more specifically, it is a reflection of my father's wisdom and discernment. Thank you both.

**David:** I believe for my father, writing this book has been the single most difficult undertaking he has experienced other than my mother having breast cancer. For two years, as my father wrote this book, his level of introspection on his methods of parenting has caused large amounts of pain and even regret. He has painstakingly attempted to expose all of his and my mother's struggles, mistakes, and imperfections as parents.

I struggle often with the way I was parented. The truth is I have the greatest parents ever. How can this be?

Reading this book will reveal many of the mistakes we make as children and how parents make even bigger mistakes dealing with them.

My father wrote this book not because he is interested in saving face but because he is interested in saving relationships between parents and their children.

**Joy:** While everyone is searching for a formula for the perfect family, this next generation of parents, many of whom are my friends and peers, needs to hear this message from my parents' experience through the insight and writing of my father. Not only will you get tons of wisdom and tips, but you will also hear stories of my parents' own mistakes. (*Twitch, twitch* . . . really, I'm fine!) And hopefully that is where the freedom will come for you as a parent as you strive not to mess your kid up too much. Remember, there is no perfect family, but this book will give you some much-needed tools for your toolbox.

As all three of our children have mentioned, I have written about the ups and downs in our parenting journey. I wanted to share our discouraging incidents to make it clear:

- There is no *perfect family*, a term that is almost an oxymoron. Immaturity, irresponsibility, and impiety guarantee imperfection.
- There is hope for you, so do not give up. Find encouragement from our stories. We call this *negative encouragement* so you can look for the positive in what God is doing in your family.
- There is a plan to parent God's way, even when our children may seek to go their own way at times. The secret is to follow this plan regardless. When you do, I believe you succeed in His eyes. This book is my humble attempt to explain His plan.

# Introduction

# Can Love & Respect Work
# When Parenting Your Kids?

We've all been there . . .

We are in the checkout line at the grocery store, struggling to get the groceries out of the cart while our five-year-old child (who definitely is old enough to know better) throws a temper tantrum because we said no to a candy bar. To make it worse, while lying on the floor kicking and screaming, Buddy blurts out loud enough for the butcher grinding hamburger in the back to hear, "You don't love me!"

Embarrassed, we pick the child up and loudly whisper in his ear, "Young man, you are being very disrespectful. Stand up and stop this. Now!" Of course, this only intensifies his crying, and by the time we make it out the door, we are totally embarrassed, defeated, and discouraged . . . again.

What is really going on here, besides the fact that Buddy did not get his way? Why do things get crazy so fast?

The same holds true when Kelli turns sixteen and wants to borrow the keys to the car but hears from mom and dad, "Not tonight, Kelli. Sorry." She grumbles, "I can't believe this. You guys don't care about me. I need the car! You said I could drive! This family hates me!"

These expressions of being unloved, uncared for, and even hated have been used by every son and daughter since the beginning of time. Our offspring seem to be born with the ability to manipulate us when they are not getting what they want, but are their complaints always manipulation? Suppose the child really does feel unloved? Sometimes it is hard to tell.

But for mom and dad, in that moment, they are wondering why their child cannot take a reasonable no for an answer. At such moments parents feel disregarded and disrespected. Why does this happen over and over again?

I want to give you a game plan for raising your kids, no matter what their age. To help you build this game plan, there are two basic principles to understand and apply to all ages and stages:

1. Kids need love.
2. Parents need respect.

The parent-child relationship is as easy, and as difficult, as love and respect.

When frustrated with an unresponsive child, a parent does not declare, "You don't love me!" Instead the parent concludes, "You are being disrespectful right now." A parent needs to feel respected, especially during conflicts. When upset, a child does not whine, "You don't respect me." Instead, a child pouts, "You don't love me." A child needs to feel loved, especially during disputes.

The good news is that when children feel loved, they are motivated to respond positively to parents, and when parents feel respected, they are energized to be lovingly affectionate with their kids. When these needs are met, good things happen in the family.

But, of course, the reverse happens all too often. An unloved child reacts negatively in a way that feels disrespectful to a parent. A disrespected parent reacts negatively in a way that feels unloving to the child. We might say that every negative action in the family has an equal and opposite negative reaction. This dynamic gives birth to the Family Crazy Cycle: without love a child reacts without respect; and without respect, a parent reacts without love.

Does the Bible address this love-need in a child, and this respect-need in parents? Yes.

Parents need and want the respect that Scripture plainly says is their due: "Honor your father and your mother" (Exodus 20:12) is one of many passages where children are clearly told to honor and respect their parents. And children need and want the love and sensitive understanding that Scripture teaches parents to give them. See Titus 2:4, Ephesians 6:4, and Colossians 3:21 for just a few examples of where parental responsibilities are mentioned or described.

As I have searched Scripture, I have found something that could serve well many parents, even revolutionize the parent-child relationship. But it's one thing to have a theological theory; it's another to make it work, especially in the daily crucible of child rearing. As every parent knows, from tots to teenagers children are not always respectful or honoring, and it is not always easy to be loving in the face of children who appear disrespectful. The obvious challenge then is: How do you show love to your preschooler, especially when he is having a meltdown right in the middle of the supermarket checkout line, leaving you to feel mortified and disrespected? Or how does a parent deal with a teenage daughter who yells, "You are the worst parent in the world" as she reacts with drama that could get her a role on Broadway?

While rearing three children, Sarah and I were there many times. I remember well what it is like to win a battle but realize I might be losing the war. As parents Sarah and I are not perfect, as she relays in this story:

> One day in conversation with our oldest son, Jonathan, he said, "Mom, you wanted a perfect family, and you didn't get it!" I was stunned. I had never said that, but I obviously had communicated it without words. Having come from a broken home and determined to do things differently, I realized at that moment I had wanted something that was impossible to attain. Tears later came as I was alone and reflected on his words. I had often asked God to compensate for my mistakes, but in return had I thought He would give me perfect children? As you will read in this book, we were not perfect parents, our children were not perfect, and there is no perfect family! Be encouraged . . . we are in this together!

> *Elijah will teach parents how to love their children. He will also teach children how to honor their parents. If that does not happen, I will come. And I will put a curse on the land.*
>
> —*Malachi 4:6* NIRV

In researching this book, I have searched the Scriptures from Genesis to Revelation for pertinent passages on parenting . . . and there are many. I share these with you, and I give plenty of personal illustrations—what I learned from my mistakes and also what went right. Be assured my adult children, now in their thirties, have signed off on everything I share—the good, the bad, and the ugly!

So what's the game plan?

This book is about the transforming power of love and respect between parent and child.

You will learn to:

- see love and respect as basic family needs
- stop the Family Crazy Cycle
- parent in six biblical ways called G-U-I-D-E-S that will energize your children
- discipline defiance and overlook childishness
- be the mature one, since parenting is for adults only
- work as a team, according to the gender of the children
- be a loving parent in God's eyes, regardless of a child's response

Parenting is a faith venture. As we parent "unto Christ" we reap God's reward, "knowing that whatever good anyone does, he will receive the same from the Lord" (Ephesians 6:8 NKJV).

Perhaps you are like a lot of parents I have talked with who feel defeated, ready at times to give up. I have written this book to help you hang in there. If your children are young, the game has a long way to go; if your children are teenagers, you still have plenty of time to improve your relationship. And if your children are grown, these truths are timeless since parents are always parents!

Love & Respect can and does work in the family. Let me show you why . . . and how.

—Emerson Eggerichs, PhD

# PART 1

# THE FAMILY
# CRAZY CYCLE

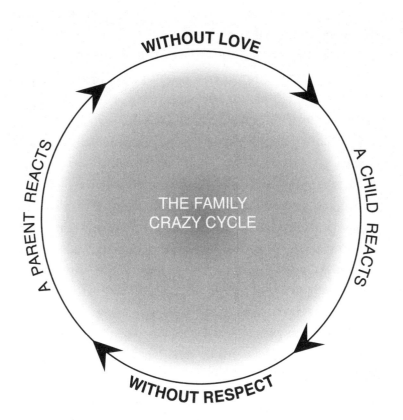

As a parent I have noticed some interesting things in the Scriptures. On one hand I saw the command to children to *honor* their father and mother. But on the other hand there is no command to them to *love* their father and mother.

In a similar way I saw that parents were not commanded to *honor* their children but were commanded to *love* their children (Titus 2:4). "Love" in this passage is *phileo*, friendship love, but there is no command to parents to *agape* a child, which is Godlike unconditional love.

I concluded that God put agape-love in the parent's heart for the sake of the child.[1] However, though a parent feels this agape-love for the child by nature, when frustrated or angry the parent can appear unfriendly (Titus 2:4), and the child can feel unloved. Then the child reacts negatively in ways that feel disrespectful to the parent.

There it was: the Family Crazy Cycle! When a child feels unloved, that child tends to react in ways that feel disrespectful to a parent. And when a parent feels disrespected, that parent tends to react in ways that feel unloving to the child. Around and around it goes, sometimes all day long . . . unless something is done to stop it.

In the first three chapters we will learn how to decode as we see a Family Crazy Cycle heating up. Possibly more important, I will share strategies for defusing situations before they become a full-fledged spin into craziness.

# 1

## IF KIDS WOULD ONLY COOPERATE, WE ALL WOULD BE GREAT PARENTS!

It was a hot summer day in 1986. We were driving home in our van from a refreshing and enjoyable vacation. All was serene as we basked in the glow of togetherness—until the last two hundred miles. Rather suddenly, Jonathan, ten; David, eight; and Joy, four, started squabbling over this and that, and despite our requests to "cease and desist," the verbal battles continued until we halted at a rest stop to eat lunch in a picnic area. We had hoped the bickering was over, but that apparently was not the case. Jonathan continued to give Joy a bad time and David just grumbled at them both. Finally, as the decibels and tension reached optimum pitch, Sarah had had enough. She rose from our picnic table and announced: "I want to quit!" Then she simply walked off and headed over to another empty picnic table to be alone. I quickly corralled the kids and herded them to the restrooms for a bathroom break.

Sarah was sitting on a picnic table and noticed a group of bikers who had stopped for a bit of shade and some favorite libations. She watched the tattooed figures with combat boots and sleeveless jean jackets get on their motorcycles, rev their engines, and then speed away. At that moment she remembers thinking, *I wonder what it would be like to ride off into the sunset and leave these parenting burdens behind?* She did not really want to abandon the family, but she recalls feeling so discouraged with being a parent that she had this irrational fleeting thought—and it scared her.

I returned with the kids, got them into the van, and then walked over to the picnic table where Sarah began sharing her feelings. The bottom line was that she had had her fill. For what seemed like an eternity of silence (it was probably about a minute), we both stared into the distance. It was time for the man of the family to speak up. I wanted to try to relieve the situation with a little humor and say something like: "Don't you dare leave by yourself! Let's go together!" But the look on Sarah's face stopped me. There was a strained silence while we headed back to the car. I could see she was really hurting at the core of her being. With shoulders drooping and tears in her eyes, she said: "It's just not working. I feel like such a failure."

I tried to give some words of comfort, but she was too numb. At that moment she felt totally defeated; and truth be told, I felt pretty much the same.

As we discussed this story recently, Sarah confessed: "Apart from telling you how I felt, I never mentioned this episode to any of my friends until many years later. I just felt too guilty for having such intense feelings of just wanting to give up."

I am sure you could match this episode from *The Eggerichs Family Crazy Cycle* with stories of your own. I recall a young mother who was attending a Family Crazy Cycle workshop I was giving. She came up afterward and told me that things had been truly crazy with her three kids earlier that day, and finally she asked her nine-year-old son, one of the chief offenders, "Do you want to meet Jesus?" Before he could answer, she added, "Because if you don't stop this, you *are* going to see Him right now!"

Of course, this mom was not really planning anything that drastic, but she was at Wit's End Corner and had to say something to send a message, just as Sarah felt when for a split second she imagined climbing on a Harley and leaving her family in the dust. We all know how it feels. If only kids would cooperate, it could be so simple.

*Kids do not always apply Proverbs 23:25: "Let your father and your mother be glad, and let her rejoice who gave birth to you."*

But every parent knows it is not that simple. Again and again parents are left trying to figure out what is really going on when a child acts up, and no matter what they do, it only seems to make him act up all the more.

So what do I suggest? First, no matter what it is—a minor or major squabble, a dramatic outburst, or maybe whining that just continues nonstop—do not be afraid to admit: "The Family Crazy Cycle is starting to spin."

Note the Family Crazy Cycle diagram on page 1: Without love (or perceiving what he thinks should be love) your child reacts negatively. When your child does not cooperate or misbehaves in any number of ways, you feel disrespected. Without respect you can (and often do) react negatively in ways that feel even more unloving to your child. Naturally, your child reacts by stepping up his disagreeable behavior—the whining, the dawdling, whatever he can do to let you know he is feeling unloved—and round and round it can go.

As for our vacation trip gone sour, I do not believe the children were feeling unloved; they were just being kids who had been cooped up in a car too long. They were siblings in typical conflict: Jonathan wanted to read his book; Joy wanted Jonathan's attention; Jonathan became irritated when Joy would not leave him alone. David became angry because as he tried to draw a picture, Joy would hit his elbow and mess up his picture.

The problem was they did not respond to our persistent efforts to get them to stop. Sarah and I definitely felt disrespected and were not quite sure how to deal with the situation. When kids do not listen to parents, at some level, parents feel disrespected.

We have since discovered that there are three questions that are helpful to ask when the Family Crazy Cycle starts to crank up:

1. Is my child feeling unloved?
2. Am I feeling disrespected?
3. How will I parent God's way regardless?

In this section on the Family Crazy Cycle, we are looking at the first two questions. We will look at that all-important third question in part 2: "The Family Energizing Cycle" and in part 3: "The Family Rewarded Cycle." So let's dig a little deeper into when and why a child might feel unloved and when and why you—the loving parent—might feel disrespected.

Concerning the first question, "Is my child feeling unloved?" I want to stress that many times a child is not necessarily feeling "unloved." It is entirely possible that he is acting this way out of childish irresponsibility, selfishness, or even open defiance. He is unhappy, he is just not getting his way, and he is letting you know it. On the other hand, there are times when, from your child's point of view, he needs some love right now, at least some attention. He may be asking for your love in a childish, clumsy way, but that is what he wants. You are his main source of love. He needs your love and is always looking for it in one way or another.

Let me illustrate. One day when she was almost five, Joy was acting whiny, claiming it was because she was sick. She wanted me to lie down with her, and while I had a lot of sermon preparation to do, I set my irritation aside and decided to do so, at least for a few minutes. As we lay there, she said, "Give me a hug." I responded: "So that's the real issue. You just needed a little love time." I will never forget her reply: "Of course, and you should know that." I gave Joy her hug, several in fact, and she was instantly "healed." A few minutes later she scampered off happily to play.

I learned something that day that helped me many other times when parenting Joy and her two brothers, David and Jonathan. I learned the importance of asking the first question: Is my child feeling unloved? But I also began to get in tune with another question that was still forming in my soul during those early years: Am I feeling disrespected? Often I knew I felt disrespected, but I was not sure if I should have these feelings since I was supposed to be the mature adult. I wondered if I was just being egotistical and touchy. Maybe the kids were just being kids, and I was too self-focused and sensitive.

> *Children just naturally do silly, careless things.*
> —Proverbs 22:15 GNT

On that first turn of the Family Crazy Cycle, when our children are acting less than positive, we must avoid the knee-jerk reaction that causes us to think: *This kid is not being respectful. Children are supposed to obey their parents. I am going to have to put a stop to this!* Parents know instinctively their children should respect them. Most parents also know the fifth commandment: "Honor your father and your mother" (Exodus 20:12). The apostle Paul echoed God's commandment in Ephesians 6:1–2 when he wrote: "Children, obey your parents. . . . HONOR YOUR FATHER AND MOTHER."

With all this scriptural backup to our parental authority, we can feel the pressure to make sure our kids are obedient, reacting too sternly, or in frustration or anger. This is an example of how parents can start the Family Crazy Cycle by overreacting to kids' just being kids. Our rigidity and negativity are perceived as unloving to our children, who then feel unfairly judged, and now we have entered the Family Crazy Cycle.

Once you admit to yourself, "Yes, I am feeling disrespected," then you can ask, "*Should* I feel disrespected?" This is a crucial question that you should not answer without thinking it through. A parent must guard against taking offense against a child who has no disrespectful intentions. Irresponsibility is not the same as disrespect. Granted, I will not deny that irresponsible actions can feel disrespectful. For example, you instruct your child to be careful with his milk cup, but somehow his little elbow knocks his cup over. It is a critical moment. You may feel disrespected. Why can't your child be more careful? But this is the right moment to repeat an old saying: "Don't cry over spilled milk!" Yes, the child made a mess, but kids will be kids. Irresponsible at times, yes, but do not confuse this with disrespect.

"But you just don't know how many messes I wipe up each day." Yes, I do. Sarah and I reared three children, all of whom had a knack for spilling their milk. Did we respond perfectly each time? No. In fact, Sarah recalls her repeated prayer: "Lord, help me respond, not react."

In fact, there are times when—just as a child may be reacting out of childishness and not because he is feeling unloved, so a parent often reacts out of impatience, frustration, and just plain exhaustion. Cleaning up one more mess of spilled milk can put us over the edge. In that moment we may not be feeling disrespected, but we are negatively reacting, nonetheless. The important thing to remember is, whether we are feeling disrespected or just fed up with cleaning up spills, our harsh reactions feel unloving to our children . . . and now we have started a Family Crazy Cycle reaction.

At those times we all need to pray that simple prayer: "Lord, help me respond, not react." Our reactions reflect our sin nature, but asking for God's help calms our hearts. As parents we need to show compassion, the kind the psalmist described when he compared the Lord's compassion to the compassion a father is to have on his children (Psalm 103:13). The Lord is our model for showing compassion.

If you saw the movie *Hook*, you may remember the scene where Peter Banning (played by Robin Williams) is on a plane with his son, Jack, and he becomes frustrated when Jack keeps irritating everyone within reach or earshot. Finally, Peter says: "What in the #%$* is the matter with you? When are you gonna stop acting like a child?" Jack responds, "But I *am* a child," and his father snaps back, "Grow up!"

While the scene is supposed to be humorous, Peter Banning was not parenting well at that moment. I had a father who was something like Robin Williams's character, and I know from personal experience how a child can be provoked and exasperated, with his parent's unloving behavior eventually deflating his spirit.

One such moment is very vivid in my mind. When I was not quite three years old, I saw my dad attempting to strangle my mom. I rushed at him and began pounding him with my little fists. He slapped me on the head, and I sank down, crying. He let go of Mom, and afterward she wept. This episode, among others, often led me to ask myself as a young child, "Does my daddy love me?"

As time went on and my dad continued to react to me in ways that felt unloving, I acted disrespectfully plenty of times. I did not understand all the dynamics of what was going on, but I was actually trying to get my dad to wake up to my need for his reassuring love. It rarely happened. My childhood years often saw my dad leaving me bewildered and feeling rejected.

As a little boy, I felt I never could do anything right. When I tried to help my dad with some project around the house but failed to do what he wanted, this bugged him to no end. I can still hear his words ringing in my ears: "You are useless! If I want anything done, I have to do it myself!"

Not surprisingly, I wet the bed until I was eleven, and I would have closed off my spirit to my dad completely had it not been for my mom. When I went to her with my hurt, frustration, and anger at my dad, she would say: "Well, your daddy doesn't know how to be a dad because when he was three months old, his daddy died. He grew up without a daddy. So he doesn't know how to do this."

Somehow that answer seemed to help me get through my childhood, but as I entered the teen years, my mother could clearly see my home life with my father was impairing my development as a young man. She pursued sending me to military school. My dad did not protest (I presume because he foresaw too many hassles with me as a teenager). From age thirteen to eighteen I attended military school, and at age sixteen, when I placed my faith in Christ as my Lord and Savior, receiving Him into my heart, I came to see and believe that God caused "all things to work together" for my good (Romans 8:28).

Because of my own hurts I am able to understand the internal struggles and needs of a child who feels unloved. My mother was very loving, and this made all the difference for me as a child, but because of how my father treated me, I can empathize with the many children who feel misunderstood and unloved and who never really intend to be disrespectful.

Unfortunately, I did not always apply that empathy as a parent. Fast-forward to when I was a pastor, speaking at a Christian summer camp. I was about to give the evening message, and my son David, who was around age ten, was misbehaving because he wanted to do something that we did not have time to do at the moment. I distinctly remember feeling: *This child is purposely defying me. He is showing me disrespect to retaliate for not getting his way.*

*You teach others— why don't you teach yourself?*
—Romans 2:21 GNT

I took David out to our car, where I hoped to reason with him. He sat in the backseat; I sat in the front. I tried to get him to talk but got only cold silence, which made me feel more and more disrespected. Finally, I angrily bawled him out for his disrespect, but that only made David more convinced I was being unfair and unloving. He stared out the window with no remorse or apology—only silence—and it ended in a stalemate. I had to speak in a few minutes, so I had David accompany me to the auditorium, where I addressed the crowd as best I could, all the while feeling like a complete hypocrite because of my horrible parenting. What is fascinating about this episode is that while I remember it vividly, David does not recall any of it whatsoever and does not believe it damaged him. It seems that our kids do not always retain much of what we guiltily dredge up from our memories, but what they do oftentimes recall as unfair or hurtful, we remember not at all. Welcome to parenting!

As I reflect on that scene where I blew it with David, it never occurred to me that he may have been feeling unloved. Perhaps he just wanted time with me and was feeling left out. If I had addressed the situation with that understanding, could this conflict have been avoided? It is hard to be sure. David could be stubborn about wanting his own way, especially at that age. But one thing is for sure: my angry outburst accusing him of being disrespectful did not help him open his heart to me.

There are many other incidents I will share of times when Sarah and I mistakenly shamed our children for what we thought was disrespect. As Sarah and I have discussed these past situations, she has observed: "I am reminded how we failed to slow down and try to decode. What I remember is that too often we reacted immediately. We did not wait to think it through and respond later. We did not take a couple of minutes to collect our thoughts and calm our emotions."

I agree. I am afraid that sometimes we would fire, then aim, then get ready. We were wired too tightly much of the time. I can remember saying, "We should deal with these situations more like my mom. She would stay quiet and thoughtful before she spoke or acted."

That night at camp with David, I could have decoded him much better, but I did not know then what I know now. What I had to learn, by trial and error, is that parenting is for adults only. As parents we need to decode the child and make the first move. Decoding is an art, and in chapter 2 we will dig a little deeper into how to go about it.

# 2

## STOPPING THE FAMILY CRAZY CYCLE, PART I

### *Decode*

When my son David was in his twenties, he umpired Little League baseball. One day a father of one of the players showed up drunk at the baseball field. It so happened his eight-year-old son lost a lens from his glasses in center field and was searching for it. As the father wandered onto the field, he began screaming at his son for losing the lens.

David called for a time-out and went out to center field along with others to look for the lens. However, the dad kept shouting threats and obscenities at his son. Then, he cocked back his fist and punched the little boy in the face. The boy went down. And the dad, still in his drunken stupor, turned around and staggered off the field before anyone had time to confront him.

The little guy lay there stunned. Then he sat up, fighting back the tears. He was determined not to cry. Immediately, David went to him. Putting his arm around him, David gently said,

"Don't worry; you didn't mean to lose it. We'll find the lens. It will be okay." The boy burst into tears.

My heart broke when David told me this, and I still tear up every time I tell the story. The minute David touched him, this little boy sobbed. His little spirit responded to love.

Do you recall what it is like to be eight? At a moment like that, this tiny boy was confused. In his little mind, he had done a bad thing in losing his lens. He knew he didn't mean to, but motives aren't understood at that age. After all, since his dad was mad, he must have been behaving badly. He had no idea what others felt. As far as he knew, they felt the same way his dad did. Oh, the insecurity this little guy must have felt at that moment.

*We need to always remember that our child is "but a youth" (1 Samuel 17:33).*

## A Deflated Spirit Is a Crushed Spirit

But what, you may ask, does this sad story have to do with decoding, the parent's first task in staying off of the Family Crazy Cycle? Surely the drunken dad was in no shape to decode anything or anyone. But I use the little boy as an example to underline how badly children need our love and how we must constantly be decoding them and the situation, even when we may feel disrespected by what is happening. Our first questions in any situation must be, "What is going on? What seems to be the issue?" The apparent issue was the lost lens from the child's glasses, but as the father started railing at his son, then striking him down, the root issue was most apparent: the little boy had the overwhelming feeling that "my daddy doesn't love me."

From feeling scared and guilty about losing his lens, the boy was jolted with much deeper pain: a crushed spirit from the screaming, a broken heart from the fist. He had been created by God to be loved, but no one loved him—so he felt. He was designed to be valued and treated as significant. So he held back his tears. If he cried, it could get worse. Everyone might turn on him. He felt so alone and scared. He wanted someone to comfort him.

Then a hand was placed on his shoulder and an arm came around him. He heard the soft voice of an adult: "Don't worry; you didn't mean to lose it. We'll find the lens. It will be okay." The boy burst into tears. It was love. It was respect. Every human spirit longs to be loved and respected, crying out, "Does anybody love me? Am I significant to anyone?"

The writer of Proverbs noted, "When the heart is sad, the spirit is broken" (Proverbs 15:13), and he also asked the poignant question: "A crushed spirit who can bear?" (Proverbs 18:14 NIV).

The story of the abused Little Leaguer captures an extreme and wicked tragedy we find hard to imagine. I tell it not because I believe you are remotely like this father, but because the little boy serves as a profound reminder of the tender, vulnerable, and precious spirit of children.

*Jesus said, "Don't be cruel to any of these little ones! I promise you that their angels are always with my Father in heaven" (Matthew 18:10–11 CEV).*

A deflated, broken spirit in children is a serious thing. In Colossians 3:21 the apostle Paul warns: "Fathers, do not exasperate your children." Why? They might "lose heart." The phrase "lose heart" is especially meaningful,[1] because it so aptly describes what happens when a child's spirit deflates. You can see it in the droop of the shoulders, the fallen countenance, the "What's the use?" expression.

You do not have to strike a child to deflate him. You can do it with harsh words, severe looks, or even well-meant admonitions like, "Why can't you get better grades, like your sister?" We must always guard against getting so angry or irritated that we cause our children to deflate in defeat—to lose heart. Their tender hearts can feel perplexed—confused about how to please us. As their spirits are quenched, eventually they close off to us. As they lose heart, we lose their hearts.

## My Mom Thought I Was Angry Enough to Kill My Dad

But a deflated spirit is not the only danger. Another manifestation of an unloved child is anger. Some kids do not deflate as often as they erupt. They fight back as though their emotional survival depends on it. As Paul has stated, some children can be provoked to anger (Ephesians 6:4), and I recall numerous times when I was provoked to anger by my father. As I look back now, I'm sure that was not his intention. He was actually a goodwilled man, but he had a volatile temper, and I had a way of irritating him on a regular basis.

One episode stands out: I came into the kitchen, where my mother was working, took a huge butcher knife from the drawer, and told her that I was going to kill Dad in the other room. Though I was making all kinds of macho noises, I was really bluffing. I was angry, but I had no intentions of killing him.

Mom, of course, had no way of knowing that I was bluffing, and she freaked out. I had never seen her in such a fearful panic before, and her traumatized look frightened me. I realized that

I had almost pushed her over the emotional edge, and when she demanded the knife from me, I handed it over.

I recall that Mom and Dad never talked to me about this episode, and I assume Mom never mentioned it to Dad. Neither said, "Son, what are you feeling inside? Do you feel we don't care about you? Talk to us." I wonder what would have happened if my dad had discerned my incensed attitude and said, "I can tell that you are upset with me. Let's talk about how I hurt and angered you. I need to seek your forgiveness." As I review that scene in my mind, I cannot recall the issue that had provoked me to anger, but it had turned into The Issue: I felt unloved, and I displayed disrespect. My dad's silence only reinforced that what I felt really didn't matter.

The child's deflated spirit mentioned in Colossians 3:21, and the child's angry spirit noted in Ephesians 6:4, are both problems,[2] but of the two, anger can have the most tragic results. Unloved children can display an inflamed spirit burning with anger, or they may hide their anger and let it simmer down deep inside, only to explode when pushed over the edge. Stories appear regularly in the news, telling of a child—often a teenager—who brings a gun to school and opens fire, randomly killing classmates and faculty. Most angry children do not go that far, but the potential is always there. Parents are not directly responsible for such carnage. As we will see in part 3: "The Family Rewarded Cycle," children can make their own choices apart from parental influence. Nonetheless, the apostle Paul clearly warned: "Fathers, do not provoke your children to anger" (Ephesians 6:4). As parents we must take this warning to heart. While we are not responsible for the sins of our children (Ezekiel 18:1–3, 20), Scripture also teaches that the sins of the fathers can affect a family down to the third and fourth generation (Exodus 20:5). How we parent does matter and can have short-term or long-term repercussions.

## Okay, Let's Lighten Up

Now that all of us are petrified by the thought of emotionally destroying our kids, sending them straight to prison and then to hell, let's take a deep breath and relax. (The good news, as my mom used to say, is that in prison they can get a Bible, whereas in school they cannot.)

> In parenting, "try to discern what is pleasing to the Lord" (Ephesians 5:10 ESV).

Incidents that can deflate or provoke our kids happen all the time. They wind up feeling unloved; we wind up feeling disrespected and like failures because we blew it again. Disappointingly, a small issue seems to grow into something much larger. When the Family Crazy Cycle begins to spin, the issue—whatever you are disagreeing about—is becoming The Issue. Remember, the first step in decoding is to *discern* what is happening at two levels:

1. What is going on in my child's heart?
2. What is going on in my heart, really?

When a child's spirit deflates or erupts, a parent must ask, "Is my child feeling unloved?" When the parent's spirit deflates or erupts, that parent must ask, "Am I feeling disrespected?"

If a child's behavior has irritated or angered his parent to any degree, the parent must try to step back, look at the situation, and ask himself, "Why does this upset me, and why is my child upset? Why has a seemingly simple issue turned into a much bigger deal?" It may start out seeming to be about making a mess, refusing to go to bed, or getting in past curfew, but it soon escalates into something else that strikes deep into the heart of the child or parent or both.

## Examples of How to Discern While Decoding

When an issue becomes The Issue, it is crucial to understand that one thing is usually going on in the spirit of the child and an entirely different thing is going on in the spirit of the parent. But the bottom line is: the child is feeling unloved and the parent is feeling disrespected. Let us look at three different scenarios to practice discerning how an issue escalates into The Issue.

When told that playtime is over and she must take a nap, a four-year-old melts down in an angry fit and runs into another room to her toy box and pulls out her teddy bear and some baby dolls. Mom chases after her, grabs her arm, and barks: "No! No more playing. You are taking a nap!" She picks up her kicking and screaming child and carries her back to her bedroom. After putting her to bed and catching her breath, the mother mumbles to herself: "Why is she so demanding all the time? Why can't she cooperate now and then?"

The issue—it is nap time and playtime must stop for now—has become The Issue: Mom feels frustrated and exhausted. And then comes a passing thought: *Why does my daughter not respect my instructions? Why doesn't she listen to me?* Meanwhile, the little four-year-old is feeling sorry for herself and shrieks from her bed, "You don't love me!" as she cries herself to sleep.

Or picture a father who scolds his ten-year-old son for throwing the baseball into the cushions on the couch. Just a few days ago he had told him not to throw baseballs in the house. When the boy claims, "I forgot," his father yells, "You did not forget! Don't lie to me, or you won't play in your Little League game this afternoon!"

When the son throws himself on the couch in a dejected and deflated manner, the issue is not about throwing the baseball in the house. The Issue is a love and respect issue, and here is why: The father is shouting at his son because there are expensive lamps next to the couch, which could be hit by the ball and shattered. He also warned his son just a few days ago, and the father does not buy the line, "I forgot." He feels his son is not being honest with him but is, instead, dishonestly driving him up the wall. Feeling disregarded and disrespected, Dad erupts. Feeling mistreated and unloved, his son deflates. Almost in tears, he lies on the couch, believing his dad is mean and has falsely accused him of lying.

One more example finds a mother yelling at her fifteen-year-old daughter for not picking up her room and the daughter yelling back even louder. By now the issue is not about the messy room. The daughter is feeling provoked because she is being treated as a little kid when she is told how to keep her own room. And mom? She is feeling totally disrespected because this is the third time this week she has reminded her daughter to straighten up her room. Her teenager is just not obeying her, yet doesn't the Bible clearly say, "Children, obey your parents"? No wonder mom is coming after her teenager, scolding her for her disrespect, and only seeming to get back more disrespect as the Family Crazy Cycle spins.

These are three typical scenes. You may have had a similar

one with your child this morning or last night. They depict what parenting seems to be all about. The first step in decoding is to pay attention to your child's deflating or erupting spirit. Next, ask yourself, "Is my child feeling unloved?" At the same time, you must be able to discern that perhaps *your* spirit is deflating or erupting as well. And as you recognize this, you ask yourself, "Am I feeling disrespected?"

## Do Not Be Afraid to Admit You Are Feeling Disrespected

As a parent, do not be embarrassed to admit, "Yes, I am indeed feeling disrespected." Some parents believe that because they are the adults, they must be in total control and never admit anything is wrong. Far better that you recognize what is happening (decode) and admit it. You *are* angry, feeling disrespected, perhaps feeling like Sarah did at that rest stop when our family vacation went south: "It just isn't working. I am a lousy parent."

Once we recognize we are on the Family Crazy Cycle, then what? Well, let's go back and look at our three examples, working back from the teenager to the preschooler.

> *The reality is, kids can be "contemptuous of parents"*
> *(2 Timothy 3:2 MSG).*

I talk frequently to parents who have gotten into conflicts with their teenagers but really are not sure why. I empathize because I remember similar times when our three kids were teenagers. You see your teen daughter (or son) go cold or bristle, and you think: *What is wrong here? Children are supposed to honor their parents, not treat them like this!* Your teenager is stepping on your toes—again.

Your first temptation is to come right back and scold her for her disrespect, but you already sense that will not work. *Now is the time to decode what is happening inside your teenager.* Now is the time to ask, "Is she being disrespectful, or immature and self-centered?" Typically, teenagers are preoccupied with their wants and desires and less interested in the wants and desires of others.

Therefore, although it may be difficult, you must step back and ask yourself, "Is my teenager acting in a typical way for this age and stage?" (In other words, are the immaturity and self-centeredness she is showing right now typical for girls her age?) If you are honest, the answer is, "Probably . . . in fact, definitely."

The next question to ask yourself is, "Can I keep my cool, or will I just automatically decide that my kid is being deliberately and spitefully disrespectful?" Take a deep breath and remind yourself that through these bouts with their parents, teenagers will eventually mature and learn to be others-centered and not so self-centered.

I admit these are not easy questions to ask when you are feeling disrespected. But if you want to deal positively with the situation and get off the Family Crazy Cycle, you must try. Just because you feel offended does not automatically mean your teenager is sending the message, "I don't respect you!" Don't immediately conclude that because the bed is unmade and clothes cover the floor, your teenager couldn't care less about what you say and think. It is far better to give her the benefit of the doubt.

To return specifically to the original illustration, the fifteen-year-old daughter may have intended to pick up the room but got distracted by a friend's text message about the cute new boy at school who is fast becoming the new love of her life. And of course, one text led to exchanging several more—all of which were far more interesting than hanging up sweaters or putting dirty laundry in the hamper. Yes, the daughter has been irresponsible (i.e., immature and self-centered) to no small degree, but that does not necessarily make her disrespectful.

Be assured I feel your pain as I remember how it was not that many years ago. When my daughter was a teenager, I was often quite sure that if the neighbor's little three-year-old ever wandered into Joy's room, she would get lost in the mess, and it would take a search-and-rescue team two days to find her. At one point I considered hammering pegs into the floor to give the impression everything was hung up. But guess what? Today, as a young, very mature and capable adult, Joy does not live that way—at least most of the time. When she comes home for Christmas, she reverts to her old ways!

> *The Bible recognizes "the sins and errors of . . . youth" (Psalm 25:7 GNT). This is a tough time for youth and parents.*

Am I saying to ignore your child's disregard for your rules? No. Obviously, when your teenager is irresponsible, immature, or self-centered, you must deal with it firmly, and as patiently as possible. If you have already made an agreement with your teen and she is aware of your expectation that she keep her room neat, you remind her of that and let her explain why she hasn't gotten around to it yet. If you have worked out consequences with your daughter, remind her of what they are (forgoing cell phone time, for example). Whether you invoke the consequences this time around is your call. (For more on dealing with irresponsibility, see chapter 7: "**D**iscipline.")

A general rule of thumb Sarah and I used was to give our teenagers every chance to grow up and operate responsibly on their own. The more you respect your teenager's growing sense of independence, the more he will feel loved. As children move into their teens, they need love, yes, but they also have a growing need for respect. Letting them know the expectations and following through on consequences is a respectful way to treat a teenager. To give in to their irresponsibility is not respectful and does not build trust between you. Teenagers soon learn to spell love R-E-S-P-E-C-T, just as you did when you were young. Don't you remember asking your parents (or at least thinking): "Why don't you respect my ideas? Why don't you trust me?" (See chapter 11: "Parenting Pink and Blue.")

What about the ten-year-old who fired his baseball into the couch cushions—again? If you have a preteen boy, you can easily put yourself into this scene. But instead of yelling and threatening to yank him from his Little League game, stop, regroup, and recognize that the Family Crazy Cycle is revving its engines. Do not let it pop the clutch and roar into action. *Decode, right on the spot.*

Yes, you reminded him of your order not to throw his baseball in the house. Did he forget your order and do it impulsively? Perhaps. Was he trying to defy you and disrespect you? Unlikely. Was what he did irresponsible—focused on his own interests and the fun in throwing the ball? Indeed! Yes, he needs a firm reprimand and disciplining, but shouting at him and telling him he is a liar will only continue the Family Crazy Cycle.

And what of the four-year-old who wanted to keep on playing and not take her nap? I tend to cut preschool moms a lot of slack at times such as these. Her runaway child demands that she give chase, catch her, and carry her back to her bed. What else can she do? Give in, give up, and let the child have her way? No, she must win this battle of wills.

Should she feel guilty because the daughter cries herself to sleep? Probably not. Should she feel disrespected because her daughter did not listen to her original request to stop playing and take a nap? Undoubtedly no. Her daughter was being four. Childish, yes. Disrespectful, no.

Was her daughter feeling unloved as she cried herself to sleep? Perhaps, but more likely she was having a pity party. Remember, she is four and a bit headstrong to boot. She likes to have her way, and not getting her way is not quite the same as being unloved.

My point is this: as you decode what is happening inside your child, do not immediately conclude he is being deliberately disrespectful when the bed is not made, the baseball is flying around the living room, or you get no cooperation on taking a nap. Whatever the age level, if you erroneously conclude this, you are certain to feel offended and outraged. In all likelihood, an angry reaction will be an overreaction. Your child will then feel unloved and react in a way that can feel even more disrespectful to you. It is at this point that the issue—being messy, tossing baseballs carelessly, not going to sleep—degenerates into The Issue, and the Family Crazy Cycle kicks into gear.

> When parenting, "If you stay calm, you are wise" (Proverbs 14:29 GNT).

## In the Heat of the Battle, Stay Cool

Your unloving reaction and your child's deflated or angry response are the two tickets to riding the Family Crazy Cycle. Talk about drama! Yes, a better approach, as your first reaction, is to assume your child is—unfortunately—being immature and self-centered, but not necessarily disrespectful. As best we can, we must not . . .

- yell at our kids for yelling
- explode in anger at our children even when they throw themselves on the floor in anger
- say, "You are the worst child in the world!" in response to being told *we* are the worst parents in the world
- lie to them about the discipline they will receive for lying
- exasperate them to the point that they lose heart (even though we feel exasperated and seem to be losing heart)
- feel sorry for ourselves in the face of their pouting and feeling sorry for themselves
- be unreasonable in the face of their unreasonableness
- match their foolish words and actions by our own lack of wisdom and patience

Here is my point: if you personalize every immature, self-centered, irresponsible action from your child as disrespect, you will be misjudging more often than not, and your rigidity will foster the Family Crazy Cycle. Out of the blue, the household seems filled with madness.

The solution is found in love and respect. We must not deprive our children of love when we feel that they deprive us of respect. Additionally, we must not be unloving to motivate them to be respectful any more than they can be disrespectful to motivate us to be loving. Parenting is definitely for adults only. We must bring our maturity to bear on the daily skirmishes in the family. In the heat of the battle, we must remain cool, calm, and collected.

Decoding is our first important job, but there is a second

vital step we must take at practically the same time. We must *defuse* the situation by doing some very obvious things to assure our children that we love them no matter what. Not always easy, but possible with God's help. I will explain why and how in the next chapter.

# 3

# STOPPING THE FAMILY CRAZY CYCLE, PART II

## *Defuse*

In chapter 2 we looked at the first step in stopping the Family Crazy Cycle: decoding what is going on both in your child and in your own spirit. We have seen how a little issue can quickly, sometimes in a split second, escalate into The Issue: the child does not feel loved, and you, more than likely, feel disrespected.

As important as decoding is, it is only the first step in stopping the Family Crazy Cycle. We have all seen the movie thrillers where the time bomb is ticking away and the hero has a few seconds to cut the right wire. Just before the final second passes, he defuses the bomb and shuts down the detonating device. Whew! Catastrophe averted!

In a real sense parents face defusing situations many times a day. We must not only decode why there is craziness in the family; we must defuse it. But what do we do to stop the negative reactions from the child or teen that unnerve the whole family?

For that matter, how do we mollify our own negativity so that we do not spark the craziness?

God wired children to need love. Unfortunately, the sin nature of our kids leads to their disrespectful reactions when feeling unloved. At these moments God calls us to try to defuse their potential wailing and shrieking. God wired parents to need respect. Unfortunately, the sin nature of parents leads to unloving reactions when feeling disrespected. We must defuse our potential rashness and our desire to bite back.

> All of us also lived among them at one time, gratifying the cravings of our sinful nature and following its desires and thoughts. Like the rest, we were by nature objects of wrath.
>
> —Ephesians 2:3 NIV

How? When you have decoded the situation and seen that the Family Crazy Cycle is revving its engines or perhaps has already started to spin, there are five steps you can take. I touched on some of these steps in chapter 2, but here they are in a sort of "game plan form" to give you a sequence to follow as you move from decoding to defusing.

- Call a time-out.
- Do not automatically assume disrespect.
- Teach Family Crazy Cycle 101.
- Reassure your child of your love.
- Allow for imperfection.

Sometimes you may go through all five of these steps. In other cases just calling a time-out may be enough. One step obviously may overlap with another, but all are useful to help you defuse the Family Crazy Cycle.

# Call a Time-Out When Craziness Is Escalating

Proverbs 17:14 describes defusing nicely: "Starting a quarrel is like breaching a dam; so drop the matter before a dispute breaks out" (NIV). When an argument or disagreement begins to heat up, stop the conflict—now! Then, after everyone calms down, revisit the issue.

As I talk to other parents and analyze our own family situations, I am convinced that many of us experience unnecessary strife in the family because we let the craziness go from bad to worse. We all have had these moments, have we not? The biblical (as well as practical) solution is to abandon the quarrel before it breaks out. A child needs to go to his room, sit in a chair, or step away somehow in order to calm down. Older children are capable of going quiet for ten minutes to regain composure, and the same is true of us as adults. When Sarah herded the complaining kids to their bedrooms for a time-out, she would sometimes utter, "I'd love to go to my room! Please, send me to my room for some peace and quiet." They never understood her wish, but every parent does, and such a time-out can prevent parental irritation from turning into infuriation.

I used to say to the kids, "We need to cool our jets." When too revved up, I knew we would not deal soundly with the issue. We all needed to calm down and talk respectfully and lovingly so we could hear each other. In using the time-out, I tried to make it clear to the kids that in a few moments we would hear everyone's concerns. We had one big rule: they had to speak in a respectful manner, and we had to talk to them lovingly. Fair is fair.

To use a word picture, our kids have a "love tank" and we have a "respect tank." Our kids have an air hose leading to their love tank. When we step on their air hose (or they think we did) they may react in disrespectful ways in the heat of the moment. Taking a time-out helps them cool off and begin to talk respectfully.

Conversely, as parents we have an air hose leading to our respect tank. When our kids stomp on our air hose, it does us no good to yell and scream when we feel unfairly treated. We need to calm down and talk lovingly to defuse the situation and keep the Family Crazy Cycle from spinning. This would be a good time to pray, "Lord, help me to respond, not react."

*A parent's "wisdom yields patience; it is to one's glory to overlook an offense," such as a child's failure to show respect (Proverbs 19:11 NIV).*

Another passage to memorize and bring to mind is Proverbs 10:12: "Hatred stirs up strife, but love covers all transgressions." Whenever air hoses are being stepped on, always remember that *you are the adult*. As the more mature one, you have a greater ability to choose between detonating the sputtering bomb of feelings *or* defusing it on the spot.

Let me ask you a rather personal question: Do you sometimes have a short fuse with the kids? Scripture tells us: "A hot-tempered man stirs up dissension, but a patient man calms a quarrel" (Proverbs 15:18 NIV). There are certainly days that can leave a normally calm, slow-to-anger parent ready to lose it at any moment. You lose self-control, which is your issue, not the kids'. They might light the fuse, but you have the choice to blow it out or just blow up and put everyone on the Family Crazy Cycle.

Truth be told, the craziness in the family intensifies and worsens because of the parents' immaturity, not the kids' immaturity. It is not that our children cause us to be angry, but rather that their actions can reveal our hot-tempered personality. We need to create a new default mode: be slow to anger, take a time-out to calm down, and defuse the craziness.

Calling time-out may be all you have to do. Sometimes it is that simple. Our two-year-old grandson, Jackson, is already learning. His mommy texted, "Jackson just handed me a piece of his train track and said, 'Broken. Batteries.' I told him it couldn't be fixed with batteries and asked him if he broke it. He said yes and that he needed a time-out. I asked, 'How long?' He said, 'Three minutes.' If only parenting were always this easy!"

> When we read, "do not be children in your thinking . . . but in your thinking be mature," we are reminded that children respond to life immaturely (1 Corinthians 14:20).

## Do Not Automatically Assume Disrespect

Of course, it is not always that easy. Suppose you have been able to call time-out, but you are still feeling pretty steamed and definitely feeling disrespected. As you cool down, you need to think the situation through. As we saw in chapter 2, your child has been irresponsible, no doubt, but that does not automatically mean your child has been disrespectful. Always remember: *irresponsible is not the same as disrespectful.*

Though our children can be stubborn and resist our instruction, we must not conclude that they are always out to get us. Kids live in the moment. They do not arise at dawn to diagram ways to get on our nerves.

We must see our kids as goodwilled though not always well behaved. Parents must continually ask themselves the question: "Is this an instance where my love should overlook the offense?"

More often than not, the answer is yes, and the Family Crazy Cycle probably will not spin.

When my sons would have brief skirmishes as children, many times I called time-out, separated them, and had them calm down. Usually, the time-out took care of the problem and ten minutes later they were back outside playing catch. When all went well, it was because I had the sense not to meddle too much in their dispute. I heeded the warning in Proverbs 26:17: "Like one who seizes a dog by the ears is a passer-by who meddles in a quarrel not his own" (NIV).

I am sure you have the picture. You would be foolish to grab a dog by the ears and yank hard. Why do it figuratively with your kids?

But I have to admit there were other times when I would foolishly crank up the Family Crazy Cycle again by jumping in during a time-out to "grab the dog by the ears." This was usually because I felt the boys were fighting in direct disregard of my instructions not to fight. I personalized their skirmish to mean my authority didn't matter. I projected onto my children my false belief that they disregarded my instruction because they were defying my leadership and rules. At those moments I slipped back to military school mode, where in my senior year I earned the rank of captain, second in command of the corps. I had leader responsibilities to drill underclassmen and see that they kept proper decorum. The cadets obeyed my orders and respected me because I had the authority to make life difficult for them if they didn't.

There were times when I subconsciously expected the same respect from my children that I had received from the cadets. I had to learn that a family is not a military school. On a particularly stressful day I would foolishly presume they were disrespecting me, when the truth was they were not thinking about me but simply arguing or fighting with each other. I read something into their misbehavior that was not there. I would make matters worse by starting to lecture one or both boys and succeeded in only reigniting the quarrel. I would forget the sage advice in Proverbs 20:3: "Keeping away from strife is an honor for a man, but any fool will quarrel."

## Teach "Family Crazy Cycle 101"

Okay, but what about the times when the kids are rowdy, careless, and rude, and you feel disrespected and react negatively, causing the kids to feel hurt and unloved? Everyone may be a little dizzy from starting to get on the Family Crazy Cycle, but is there nothing positive you can do? Yes, there is. Now is a perfect time to teach your kids the basics of "Family Crazy Cycle 101."

First, defuse the craziness by apologizing for losing your cool and then comment, "You know, we just went on the Family Crazy Cycle." Next, in whatever language works with your child, explain that without love a child reacts without respect, and without respect a parent reacts without love. The result is the Family Crazy Cycle and nobody is happy.

*No one knows when the age of accountability begins, but we do know that "children" can be "too young to know right from wrong" (Deuteronomy 1:39 GNT).*

How old should children be when you start teaching them how the Family Crazy Cycle works? My personal opinion is that they should be able to reason with their parents and explain their motives. Many kids are ready by age six or seven; others may take a little longer.

You know your children and will be able to tell. If your children are already teenagers or even young adults, gender differences in how they relate to one another also becomes an essential piece of the relationship puzzle. Our sons can speak harshly and abruptly to their sisters in ways that feel unloving, and our daughters can push their brothers' buttons by using disrespectful words and a condescending tone. Both need to grasp that it is not just what they say but how they say it that makes things crazy between them (see chapter 11: "Parenting Pink and Blue").

When teaching your kids rudiments of the Family Crazy Cycle, begin by explaining that when they feel out of sorts and are having a bad day, it can get them upset and irritated—and feeling unloved. They can say or do things that appear rude and disrespectful, which in turn upset those around them, who then end up feeling unloved or disrespected. Sometimes you may get strict with them and sound like you do not care about how they feel, which only makes them feel worse, so they come back with more rudeness and anger, and around and around you all can go on the Family Crazy Cycle.

Then go on to say that they can team up with you to stop the craziness. They can grasp the idea that sometimes we appear to be rude, disrespectful, or unloving when we do not mean to be that way at all.

Our kids are able to understand that parents and children can "step on each other's air hose" without meaning to do so. Their air hose leads to a "love tank"; our air hose leads to a "respect tank." They need love like they need air to breathe; we need respect in the same way. When we do not get enough love or respect, we can cross the line and begin talking in disrespectful or unloving ways, and the Family Crazy Cycle spins.

As we get these ideas across, we can ask the child, "How can we stop the Family Crazy Cycle once it starts spinning?" Children like to offer solutions. You will be surprised with what they come up with.

With older children we can say something like: "I find it tough to respond to your concern when you appear rude. Let's calm down and address what is happening here. I need you to talk to me respectfully. I don't want either of us to get crazy. Are you ready to talk respectfully so I can hear your heart?" They can learn to reassure us of their goodwill and soften their negativity.

One mom helped her kids apply respect talk to their sibling relationships as well. She wrote:

> Our three youngest children are very close in age and often argue over very silly things. I sat the boys and Amy down one day and told them about the Family Crazy Cycle. We talked for about ten minutes, which is about a million-billion years in kid-time. This morning my son Isaiah said, "Mom, me and Ethan are on the happy cycle. We keep being nice to each other." He went on to say that sometimes he was nice only because he wanted to be "more mature" than Ethan. I chuckled a little and told him that was okay; sometimes I do the same thing.

Teaching your kids about the Family Crazy Cycle and how love and respect can stop or at least slow it down is not done in a day. In fact, it is something you will need to do continually as they grow from preschool up through high school and beyond. In this sense, see yourself as a coach who will repeat the information and practice these skills.

# Reassure Your Child of Your Love

We know our love for our children is still strong, but in the moment they may not feel that love. Especially with young children, we can frighten them to the core and not realize it. Kids are sensitive and can interpret our negative reaction as resenting, even hating, them. We know we would die for our kids, but they might be thinking we have plans to get rid of them if we could.

*"As a mother comforts her child," all parents must give assurance to their kids (Isaiah 66:13 NIV).*

Do I give too much weight to a parent's possible negative reactions? Perhaps. But do not forget that defusing is basically a negative process that we are trying to make as positive as possible. Kids are auditory and trusting, which means they believe what they hear. It's important when we have to reprimand them that we verbally and physically reassure them of our love. Such reassurances of love defuse the Family Crazy Cycle quite quickly, especially for younger children.

As Abba Father reassures us of His love, we must reassure our children of our love. We need to follow His example in Romans 8 when He inspired Paul to write: "If God is for us, who is against us?" (v. 31); "in all these things we overwhelmingly conquer through Him who loved us" (v. 37); and that nothing "will be able to separate us from the love of God, which is in Christ Jesus our Lord" (v. 39). God's words to us matter; so should our words to our children.

But a question remains. When reassuring our children of our love, should we suppress our honest feelings? I believe we can communicate our frustration in a controlled manner peppered with reassuring words of love. In fact, when we declare our love, this softens us. These words affect our spirit, preventing a loss of control. For example, we can look them in the eye and say with real feeling,

> "Though I love you a ton, I am upset over your ignoring me after I told you what needed to be done."

> "Look, you know I love you, but what you did is unacceptable."

> "I love you, but I am very disappointed. You didn't make your bed, get dressed, or come to breakfast on time. This is the third day in a row. Go back upstairs, make your bed, and get dressed. I'm sorry, but you'll have to eat your eggs cold."

But let's face it. No matter how hard we try to temper negativity, our children can get offended. And sometimes we just plain blow it. At those times, an apology from parent to child can heal the offense, as this dad's letter beautifully illustrates:

When my son was about four, he wanted to help me dish the ice cream for dessert. I wasn't enthusiastic because the ice cream was hard. But I stood him on a stool at the kitchen counter, opened the carton, and handed him the scoop. He pushed but couldn't get it very deep, and trying to move the scoop down and across, a partial scoop of ice cream went flying across the room and landed on the floor. I impatiently took the scoop from his hand, made some "I knew this would happen" comment, and proceeded to do it myself. Without a word, he got down off the stool and walked into the living

room, acting as if he didn't care. But the Lord helped me realize that I should have let him hold the scoop and put my hand
over his and helped him. I went to him immediately and apologized, explaining that I'd been wrong. He burst into tears,
threw his arms around my neck, and forgave me.[1]

Technically, this dad and his son were not on the Family
Crazy Cycle, or were they? We see the buildup of emotional pain
in the boy, which burst out when his dad apologized. Dad not
only defused the situation; he drained the hurt and negativity
out of his son's heart. An apology is heart surgery.

When we blow it as parents, we owe an apology to two parties: our children and the Lord. We hurt the heart of our heavenly
Father when we fail to parent as He calls us to parent. We can
confess our inadequacies to Him and then apologize to the children. For example, when we provoke our children to anger or
exasperate them to the point they become discouraged and lose
heart (Ephesians 6:4; Colossians 3:21), we should seek their
forgiveness, right on the heels of telling the Lord that we blew
it—again.

The good news is that our heavenly Father is forgiving, and
so are our children. One dad wrote, "Most of the mistakes parents make can and will be forgiven by the child, if the child
perceives sincere love from the parent." The important thing is
that we offer forgiveness as we ask for it. We know kids may
appear disrespectful without intending to be. We must be sure
we do not hang on to any offense we may have felt for their misbehavior. We must move on. If we harbor hidden feelings, we
simply feed the craziness with our unforgiving spirit toward our
kids, who are, after all, just being kids.

# Allow for Imperfection

As I have gone through my defusing game plan, you may have been thinking, *Well, all that sounds good, Emerson . . . wish it were always that simple, but what about when my kid just doesn't want to listen . . . when he is definitely being disrespectful . . . when defusing just isn't working?*

My son Jonathan mentioned during the writing of this book, "I remember us kids being nightmares."

I replied, "Yes, and Mom and I wished at times it was just a bad dream."

But the bad dream is real. Kids will be kids—every day and in every way. I admit defusing will not always work, not only because of a child's immaturity but also because of his uncooperative and sinful heart. In Jesus' parable of the prodigal son, the father tries to defuse things with the older brother, who gets angry and jealous when dad throws a party for his younger brother, complete with fatted calf, music, and dancing. The older son sulks in an attitude of defiance. He has obediently stuck with his father, faithfully done his work every day for years, but not once has he had a party. Now his whoremongering little brother comes home in disgrace and gets a hero's welcome. Despite his father's pleas, the older brother defiantly refuses to join the party. It is all just too unfair! It would seem that all dad has managed to do is fuel the flames of craziness, making him a failure as a parent.

*Childhood can be a tough time, which is why the psalmist prayed, "Remember not the sins of my youth and my rebellious ways" (Psalm 25:7 NIV).*

I don't agree. The father has acted with love. He has always loved both sons and continues to do so. But he has to rejoice because one was "dead and has begun to live, and was lost and has been found" (Luke 15:32).

Jesus' parable dramatically underscores a truth all parents know: kids are willful creatures, fully prepared to arch their backs and stick out their tongues. We must realize this is their issue. Yes, we can try to give the benefit of the doubt and not label our children as disrespectful, but when we try to calm them down, they get more negative and in fact *are* disrespectful. We can try to reassure them of our love, apologize for being unloving, and ask forgiveness, but they are having none of it, preferring to remain in a disrespectful, unforgiving mode. At best there is still tension. The Family Crazy Cycle may not be spinning out of control, but the fuse still sputters.

While working on this chapter, I asked each of my children, "Can you recall a time when you were feeling neglected, mis-understood, stupid, out-of-control, or discouraged and Mom or I failed to defuse the situation?"

Joy replied, "I would be in the midst of really being frus-trated over something, and you would ask a rhetorical question like: 'Why don't we all give thanks?' At moments like that I just wanted to throw something through the window!"

Jonathan responded, "Regardless of what you said or did, there were many moments when I felt like the worst sinner in the world, and if you only knew, you would hate me. I equated God's knowledge of me with your knowledge. I would feel shame that overwhelmed me, and for a period I hardened my heart. I can remember despising myself and fearing you guys and God, wishing I had never been born a pastor's son and yet knowing that your love was unconditional."

David recalled that tension remained numerous times because he still "felt misunderstood."

These comments illustrate that no matter how lovingly or sincerely we seek to defuse negativity, it does not always work. We overdo it, misapply it, or just fail to see what our children really need. And they often do not quite know themselves, or they may be unprepared or unwilling to receive our sage advice. As we raised our children, I don't think one day went by without some kind of flare-up taking place.

The sinful nature—theirs and ours—will display itself on a regular basis and turn into squabbles, disagreements, misunderstandings, or all-out Family Crazy Cycle behavior that has to be defused. Sarah and I can say from experience as parents, we can be wired way too tightly, and our ideals are so demanding that we do not stay relaxed and calm enough when the imperfect moments arise.

Let's face it. Paradise is lost. Having a perfect family is not in the earthly cards. And even if we could attain perfection, would we be satisfied? I wonder. Eve had Paradise, yet she wanted still more, and we all have paid the price ever since.

This does not make us bad parents but simply underscores that every child needs the Savior who died for sin because every child has a sinful nature and acts sinfully. The good news is that God uses negative moments to speak to our children's hearts about their rebellious and stubborn nature.

Sarah remembers feeling guilty as a little girl for her attitude toward her single-parenting mom. Her conscience opened her eyes to her need for the Savior. Rest assured the Holy Spirit is always at work and the conscience will speak according to God's perfect timing. You never know when your child may finally see his need for the Lord Jesus.

Meanwhile, the parenting process goes on, and when disrespect is clearly the problem, we must move to Plan D—meaning Discipline, which I define as a positive process, not a negative one. There is often a fine line between defusing and discipline, and you may go back and forth many times a day. You try to defuse the situation, but when your children simply will not comply with your clearly stated rules and are being deliberately disrespectful, you must confront them, correct them, and when necessary, follow up with logical, sensible consequences. And again, just as with many defusing situations, you reaffirm them with your love and reward obedience when it is applicable (see chapter 7: "Discipline").

## You Can Move from Defusing to Energizing

Should we despair? Should we give up? Absolutely not. We never throw in the towel . . . never! The most successful parents recognize that on average they take three steps forward and one back. They know that though they fall, they can get back up. They understand that as they allow for imperfection, they are able to move closer to their ideal, not away from it.

Understanding the Family Crazy Cycle and how to decode and defuse will bring more peace to your home. But things can get even better than that! It is possible to move from being on the defense against the Family Crazy Cycle to the offense by energizing your family with love and respect. In part 2: "The Family Energizing Cycle"—we'll explain how.

# THE FAMILY
# ENERGIZING CYCLE

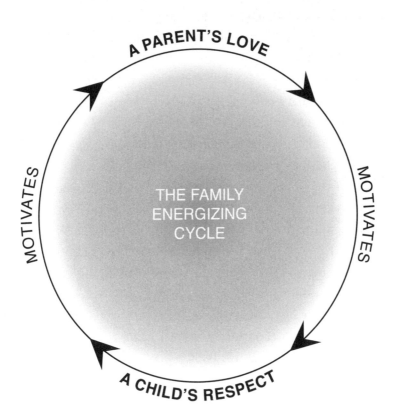

A PARENT'S LOVE

MOTIVATES

THE FAMILY
ENERGIZING
CYCLE

MOTIVATES

A CHILD'S RESPECT

In these next chapters I want to show you how to use the power of Love & Respect to get your family on the Energizing Cycle. The Energizing Cycle declares: a parent's love motivates a child's respect and a child's respect motivates a parent's love.

It is no accident that one of the Ten Commandments instructs children to honor father and mother. "Honor" is another word for "respect." If anything motivates a parent to love a child, it is receiving that child's respect. And naturally enough, God has put it in the hearts of children to respond to the positive love of their parents. As we will show, to get the Energizing Cycle rolling and to keep it humming, most of the responsibility falls on the parent to influence and energize the parent-child relationship. We are the mature ones.

To show how to parent God's way, as set forth in the Bible, I use the acronym G-U-I-D-E-S:

Give, so that a child's basic needs can be met (Matthew 7:9–11; 2 Corinthians 12:14).

Understand, so that a child is not provoked or exasperated (Ephesians 6:4; Colossians 3:21).

Instruct, so that your child can know and apply God's wisdom (Proverbs 4:1; Ephesians 6:4b; 2 Timothy 3:15).

Discipline, so that your child can correct poor choices (1 Kings 1:5–6a; Ephesians 6:4b; Hebrews 12:9).

Encourage, so that your child can develop God-given gifts (1 Thessalonians 2:11).

Supplicate in prayer, so that your child can experience God's touch and truth (2 Samuel 12:16; 1 Chronicles 29:19; Matthew 19:13, 19).

Applying G-U-I-D-E-S energizes and motivates a child—most of the time. Let's find out why.

# 4

## GIVE

## *Not Too Little, Not Too Much*

To love your children using G-U-I-D-E-S:

On Christmas morning when I was eight, I went into the living room, where the presents surrounded the Christmas tree. My eye immediately caught sight of a robot! Yes, a robot, sparkling shiny and silver, just about my height. My mind raced a hundred miles an hour. Where was the control, so I could make it walk, talk, and perform any task I desired?

I then saw that my robot was wrapped in cellophane and that it had a cardboard box head and cardboard arms. "Unwrap it," my mom urged excitedly, but I didn't want to unwrap it. I had a robot! Then she said, "Your present is underneath the wrapping."

Little did she know how disappointing her words sounded to me. Then, as I inspected my robot, I saw it. A snow sled. Mom had cleverly attached a box to look like a head, and cardboard arms to the sled handles, creating a robot-looking object. My imagination had done the rest. Before Mom's eyes, my spirit deflated like a punctured balloon. I wanted a real, moving robot with an on-off switch, not a dumb sled. My face fell, and I know my unhappiness made Mom unhappy. From then on Mom made sure she did not do anything to raise my expectations beyond reality.

That Christmas morning I learned a painful lesson: you don't always get what you want. It is a lesson all parents must teach their children. They cannot always have what they want, nor should they always get what they want. Too much of a good thing is no longer good. As Proverbs 25:16 says, "Have you found honey? Eat only what you need, that you not have it in excess and vomit it."

> *Children shouldn't have to provide for their parents, but parents should provide for their children.*
> —2 Corinthians 12:14 GW

Solomon vividly reinforced what we all know: there is a real difference between what we need and what we want. And parents also know that giving to a child's needs is a lot less complicated than trying to satisfy a child's wants. Even parents who have little or nothing want to give their children what they need—the basics of food, clothes, shelter, and health care. God has put it in the hearts of parents to give to their kids, and we all know the heartbreak it can cause when parents do not follow their God-given instincts and meet their responsibilities.

Giving is at the heart of Jesus' teaching. Do you remember when He encouraged His disciples to keep asking, seeking, and knocking on God's door with their requests? So sure could they be that their heavenly Father would answer that He used a comparison they were sure to understand: "Now suppose one of you fathers is asked by his son for a fish; he will not give him a snake instead of a fish, will he? Or if he is asked for an egg, he will not give him a scorpion, will he?" (Luke 11:11–12).

Jesus expected no reply to these rhetorical questions. He knew that His listeners recognized the universal truth about parents: they give their children what they need, not something poisonous or harmful. Parents feel duty-bound to meet the necessities, doing so with a tender moment-by-moment mindfulness. (Of course, parenting can wear you down. You give your first child perfect care, sterilizing the dropped pacifier in boiling water . . . by the fourth child you just wipe it off on your jeans—once.)

Scripture often speaks of care and compassion with parental analogies. For example: "Can a woman forget her nursing child and have no compassion on the son of her womb?" (Isaiah 49:15). Paul spoke of giving gentle care to the Thessalonians "as a nursing mother tenderly cares for her own children" (1 Thessalonians 2:7).

Unfortunately, parental love does not always function normally. Some parents do neglect their children, causing them to feel abandoned and unloved. We try to tell ourselves that such behavior is only typical of unbelievers, but not necessarily. When I pastored in East Lansing, Michigan, I heard from a college student at Michigan State University whose parents divorced when he was very young. His father moved to the other side of the country and never contacted any of the family, while his mother did her best as a single parent. As the boy grew up, they lived a dollar above poverty, just managing to scrape by. What devastated this young man was his later discovery that his dad found Christ soon after moving away, made good money, and eventually taught a huge Sunday school class with his new wife. In bitter dismay, the college student asked me, "How could he believe in God and neglect me and my needs?"

How indeed? The apostle Paul had strong words for a person who neglects family: "But if anyone does not provide for his own, and especially for those of his household, he has denied the faith and is worse than an unbeliever" (1 Timothy 5:8). Paul is saying that the would-be follower of Christ who fails to provide for his family is worse than an infidel. When we fail to meet the needs of our household, we deny the very faith we claim to hold.

Some good friends of ours hit upon hard times. When I asked how the husband was doing, the wife wrote back, "God has provided and helped us so much financially by Jeff washing windows . . . something neither of us saw him doing, but I am thankful for a husband who puts aside his pride and does what is needed for our family. It is hard to believe he is a guy with a college degree and a master's and this is where he is, but God knows, and we will trust in that for now."

Jeff did what he had to do. The true follower of Christ has no other option.

## Parents Are to Give to Needs, but What About Those Wants?

About now you may be thinking: *Okay, Emerson, I get it. Giving to a child's needs is basic, and I am committed to doing that, but what about those wants? There is a big difference between needs, which are simply not negotiable, and wants, which are very negotiable indeed. In fact, my kids have a way of negotiating their wants into needs every time!*

I understand this struggle. Kids are outstanding negotiators, which is why we need to be clear on what we believe about giving, or we can be too easily persuaded. As any parent knows, you can spoil a child, and as *The Message* paraphrases Proverbs 29:15: "spoiled adolescents embarrass their parents." In fact, they do not have to be that old. Spoiled children of just about any age can embarrass their parents, not to mention drive them crazy.

So perhaps the first question we need to ask is, "Why am I giving to my child's wants? What is my purpose?" For example, am I giving in to my child because I believe it is unloving or unkind to say no? That will spoil them for sure.

At the end of the day you must do what seems best (review Hebrews 12:10). Saying yes to what a child wants can be a loving act, but in certain cases it may be more loving to say no in order to teach the child to delay gratification and prepare him for real life. As I learned that Christmas morning when I was eight, we cannot always have what we want.

There are, of course, appropriate and reasonable times to give to your child's wants. As you give to your child wisely, he will feel loved and more energized to show you respect. Following are some good reasons to give to your children's wants.

*First, we give to show our love and spirit of generosity.* A man wrote to me about how his family did not have much when he was growing up, but his dad made the most of it: "Every once in a while he would take the family on 'surprise outings.' Usually it was to the Dairy Queen or a family movie. He would only tell us to get in the car. We didn't find out where we were going until we got there. Also, occasionally on Saturday mornings he would ask if my brother and I would like to go bowling or play putt-putt golf or something. These were good times together, just the three of us."

This man's story embodies an important principle for all parents: let a spirit of generosity engender a sense of family, which indeed leads to "good times together." A spirit of generosity usually produces reciprocity, where both sides feel loved, respected, and refreshed. As Proverbs 11:25 puts it, "A generous man will prosper; he who refreshes others will himself be refreshed" (NIV).

There are all kinds of ways to give to your kids. You can be creative and full of surprises, or you can just do something simple. In fact, the gift of time with your child is the greatest gift of all. Your gifts need not cost a penny. A trip to the park or going on a hike together can be a priceless gift. The important thing is that your giving says, "I love you because I love you because I love you!"

When I was nine, my mother taught acrobatics and tap dancing and had extra cash as a result. After payday she would sometimes come in my room and say to me, "Here. I have this dollar bill I don't want. No, I have another dollar that I don't want. Oh, I have another one." One time she did this up to eighteen dollars as we both laughed. I recall that laughter. I felt connected to her. This was apart from Christmas and birthdays; it was simply a just-because-I-love-you moment.

*Second, we can give to motivate our children to show us respect.* I'm not talking about bribing them. I mean giving to them graciously and lovingly and then appealing to them to respectfully express thanks. Though we cannot coerce their innermost gratefulness and respect, we can make that appeal. We can say to them, "I give to you because I want to give to you. However, I want you to learn to respond with respect to those who give to you and to truly be grateful."

As you teach your children to show respect for what you give them, you can set a powerful example in the respect you show to God for what He has given you. Sometimes as I take time to just bask in God's goodness, I say to Abba Father, "How can I ignore You and fail to thank You when You keep giving so lovingly to me? Thank You, Lord, for being so good to me. Forgive me for the times I am not good to You. Help me live in appreciation for Your many gifts."

Over the years I have tried to convey my attitude of gratitude to our children, to let them know in every way I can that "every good and perfect gift is from above, coming down from the Father of the heavenly lights" (James 1:17 NIV). As God gives to us, our children can observe our deep gratefulness to Him and, hopefully, develop a similar attitude. For example, when we thank the Lord for our evening meal, our children can hear our hearts express an authentic thankfulness for not only the food but also the many blessings that have fallen on us. Perhaps we will see them thanking God from their hearts as well.

I also believe that as we give to our children, our spirit of gratitude and giving can motivate them not to sin. A young man in his twenties said to me, "In my teens, I could not pursue a life of sin because I knew it would break the hearts of my good and loving grandparents and parents. They were so kind and generous that I could not bear the thought of acting in a way that would disregard and denigrate them. They had made so many deposits in me, how could I make such a huge withdrawal from them?" The young man showed respect because he understood respect and where it comes from. Again, there is no such guarantee that a child will respond this way, but our spirit of generosity tends to spawn such attitudes.

*Third, our generous giving helps our kids discover their worth to us and God.* They need to hear us say we give to them not because they deserve our gifts, but because we place immeasurable value on them. From there, we can make the case that Jesus made about our heavenly Father: "Look at the birds of the air; they do not sow or reap or store away in barns, and yet your heavenly Father feeds them. Are you not much more valuable than they?" (Matthew 6:26 NIV).

But (and it is a big *but*) can we give with good intentions to keep the family on the Family Energizing Cycle and wind up spoiling our kids anyway? Of course. Giving anyone—adult or child—anything includes the risk of under-mining their spiritual fiber and character. As Moses taught the Law to the Israelites in the wilderness, he kept warning them to impress it on their hearts and the hearts of their children. He did not want them to forget God once they reached the Promised Land of milk and honey and started enjoy-ing houses they did not build, wells they did not dig, and vineyards and olive groves they did not plant (Deuteronomy 6:1–12; 8:7–14). Being spoiled is no help in remembering God and His will for your life.

*I warned you when you were prosperous, but you replied, "Don't bother me." You have been that way since childhood— you simply will not obey me!*
—Jeremiah 22:21 NLT

Too much giving can make children extremely selfish. Proverbs 30:15 tells us "the leech has two daughters," named "Give" and "Give." We must guard against our children becom-ing "slaves, not of our Lord Christ but of their own appetites" (Romans 16:18).

When we indulge our children, they are apt to see us not as loving parents but as a genie in a bottle, ready to grant their wishes on command. They may give superficial respect to get more goodies, but when they do not get what they want their *respect* dissolves. The Israelites "reveled" in God's "great good-ness," but ended up rebelling against Him (Nehemiah 9:25–26). Our children can do the same thing. How sad and ironic when parental generosity results in egocentric and badly behaved kids.

At the very least, most kids know how to maneuver. If yelling and screaming don't do it, creative manipulation might. You may have heard a story similar to this eleven-year-old who asked her mother for ten dollars to give to a friend on her basketball team. She told her mom, "Her mother left the family for another man two years before, and she lives alone with her dad." Touched by her daughter's kindness, mom quickly pulled out a ten-dollar bill, saying: "There you are, honey. But tell me. Is your friend always short of money?" "Oh," replied her daughter, "only if she doesn't make enough extra spending money from selling the jewelry she gets from her dad's gift shop at the mall."

## The Foundational Principle: Doing What Seems Best

Because none of us intend to spoil our children, is there a formula to follow to avoid giving too much? Is there a surefire way to know if we should or should not give them an iPhone, a Blizzard from Dairy Queen, Nike Hyperdunks, or an all-expenses-paid education at an exclusive college, where tuition is not just off the charts but in the next galaxy? No, I do not believe there is a formula, but there is a biblical principle: "While we were children, our parents did what *seemed* best to them. But God is doing what *is* best for us, training us to live God's holy best" (Hebrews 12:10 MSG).

Yes, there is a certain amount of guesswork in parenting, but I believe Hebrews 12:10 is assuring us who follow Christ that we can trust Him to guide us in doing what is best as we try to sort out a sometimes bewildering array of decisions that seem to pop up daily concerning our kids. As the Lord trains us in what He knows is best, He trusts us to use a certain amount of plain old common sense as we seek to train our kids.

So as we seek to give to our kids "what seems best," we must sort out the needs and the wants and make some decisions. Note that Hebrews 12:10 says, "Our fathers disciplined us . . . as *they* thought best" (NIV, italics mine). Always, parents are to make the decisions, not the kids, who have an amazing ability to turn a want into a need!

Your children may protest when you decide contrary to their wants, and they may act in ways that feel disrespectful. A favorite approach is the guilt trip: "You are being unfair, cruel, and selfish." Keep in mind that in the vast majority of cases, you are not being selfish; your children are. You do not have to defer to what your kids prefer. They may accuse you of being the worst parent in the world, but there is nothing morally wrong with saying no. You are calling the shots, according to "what seems best"—for the children, the entire family, and sometimes beyond.

I love what one young man told me: "My parents cared about my physical needs. They were giving people, who displayed a spirit of generosity even when funds were limited. At the same time, they firmly said no when what I wanted wasn't what I needed."

This young man was able to accept no from his parents, but a lot of kids are not. So what do you say to the child who bellows, "You never give me anything! You are the worst parent on the planet!"? There is no absolute answer for this; it depends on the parents and how they interact with their children. When I heard this kind of comment from one of my kids, I would say, "If I am the worst parent in the world, then I am number one, and I always wanted to be number one at something. Thank you!" Somehow this worked with our kids. They were not sure if I was being sarcastic or if I actually was happy about being called "worst parent on earth," so they were rather speechless.

Another approach to the worst-parent-in-the-world charge

was one given to me by a mother who said, "Honestly, I don't think I would respond at all to that. The child knows this is over the top, and I would let him sit with his statement. I can't think of a response that wouldn't drag the parent into a futile argument. Later, when the child is calmed down, I may revisit this statement."

Whenever kids make over-the-top remarks, the key is not to lose your cool. You know you are not the worst parent in the world, and your child does too. If nothing else, say: "Sorry you feel that way. You still can't go, and I am saying no because I love you."

Above all, you should say no if you are frequently saying yes to manipulate the child and win his favor . . . in other words, bribery. I heard of one mother who frequently came home from work with a gift for her daughter, and whenever they went out, she bought her what she wanted. This mother gave to be liked and to keep her daughter happy. But bribery only guarantees a manipulated and spoiled child. It never produces genuine love, friendship, or happiness. The Preacher put it plainly: "a bribe corrupts the heart" (Ecclesiastes 7:7).

Granted, it is sometimes very tempting to say yes, just to have some peace. Kids are adept at crying long and yelling loud to get what they want. At age fifteen, one daughter confessed that it was quite simple to get from her father what she wanted: "Through the years all I needed to do was cry long enough and yell loud enough and Dad would give me what I wanted. He feared conflict with me so he gave in, and I knew that he'd give in, so I kept at him, but I was wrong for doing that."

This girl's candid confession is a good example of how a selfish, demanding child will calm down after getting what she wants. Parents who give in to this are looking for peace, but such peace is temporary. The child knows how to play the game. She has learned how to be gratified *now*, so she calms down . . . until the next time. You will pay the same price every time you enter any store with things your child wants because you always feed the selfishness instead of starving it.

If you are tired of this game, change your tactics. Instead of just waiting for the next scene in the toy department, where you will be manipulated again, make it a priority to teach your child how to delay gratification. Before heading off, have a brief talk and explain the rules: no begging for toys or other stuff she thinks she may want; otherwise, there will be consequences. Then go about your day, and when you and your child arrive at a store full of "wants," guess what your child will do? Test you, of course. When the begging and whining begin, you will say no, *and stick to it*. If the begging continues, leave the store and go home to award the child a consequence. (For more on consequences, see chapter 7: "Discipline.") Trust me. The real gift you can give your child is not gratification, by getting another toy, but learning to *delay* gratification by *not* getting what she wants. Remember, if your child lacks self-control, it is you who is being controlled.

## Give Without Playing Favorites

Be honest. Although most of us would say we love our children equally, we may "like" one child more than another during various ages and stages. If one rubs you the wrong way right now, you must strive not to be unjust and give this child less. If one child is easier to like, you must stay on guard against showing him favoritism.

Beware. Favoritism will not produce a closer relationship with the one you favor since the "favorite" knows deep down that you do not operate justly. Not only will the favored child take advantage of your favoritism but he will learn to distrust your character flaw. Truly, playing favorites can be a double whammy.

In addition, favoritism destroys sibling relationships. When Isaac favored Esau and Rebekah favored Jacob, it caused deep enmity between these two brothers, not to mention the trouble each brother had with the parent who did not favor him (Genesis 25:19–28:9). And when Jacob favored Joseph above his brothers, symbolized by giving him the coat of many colors, it led to Joseph's being sold into slavery and years of heartache for everyone involved (Genesis 37).[1]

> We need to remind ourselves of such promises: "You can be sure that God will take care of everything you need, his generosity exceeding even yours in the glory that pours from Jesus" (Philippians 4:19 MSG).

Keep in mind, you can play favorites consciously or unconsciously. You must take situations as they come. For example, I am not talking about rightly depriving a child of a privilege due to disobedience and justly rewarding another child for obedience. I mean showing partiality and discrimination of any kind on a long-term basis. Favoritism is a horrible and unfair judgment against the inner worth of the un-favored child and a betrayal of the character of the favored one.

Use Jesus as your model. Although He had His intimates among the disciples, He did not play favorites. He loved them all equally. Take note also of what Paul told Timothy about how to lead his flock in various practical matters: "keep these instructions without partiality, and . . . do nothing out of favoritism" (1 Timothy 5:21 NIV).

Give is the first step in guiding your children toward God.

Much of your children's future happiness lies in learning how to be content, and they will learn this in great part by watching their parents go without or choose to go without for good reason. From age four to adulthood my wife, Sarah, grew up in a cracker-box house as her mother, Martha, struggled to raise her children on her limited income after an unwanted divorce. Martha did not complain, nor did she compromise her belief in Proverbs 3:9: "Honor the LORD from your wealth and from the first of all your produce."

Sarah vividly recalls watching her mom tithe, giving 10 percent off the top of every meager paycheck, and then exclaim: "There! All the bills are paid for this month. Praise the Lord! I have a nickel left over, and I can buy a cup of coffee at work." As a child Sarah did not realize she was considered poor. She just learned to deal with adversity and adapted her mother's joyful spirit of contentment with what she had. Martha left her daughter an inheritance greater than money; she imparted how to trust God to give to her and how to give back to God as a grateful believer.

As you sort out giving to needs and wants in your family, keep in mind that the best thing we can give to our children is the intangible example of faith in God to supply all their needs according to His riches in Christ Jesus. You cannot give your children any greater gift than that!

For more information on the following topics, go to www.loveandrespect.com/parent/giving:

- The best way to say no
- Giving related to the gender of the child
- Giving as a parenting team

# 5

## Understand

## *Put Yourself in Their Shoes*

To love your children using G-U-I-D-E-S:
Like most parents, Sarah and I "learned on the job," and that certainly includes the next letter in our G-U-I-D-E-S acronym: **U**nderstanding. When our son David was in fifth grade, we both struggled to understand his disinterest in talking to us and sharing his heart so we could give him all kinds of wonderful advice and wisdom. Sarah recalls picking him up from the first day of school and asking, "How was your day?"

"Good."

"What did you do?"

"Nothing."

"Anything exciting happen?"

"No."

On the second day of school it was more of the same.

"David, how was your day?"

"Good."

"What did you do?"

"Nothing."

"Anything exciting happen?"

"Nah."

Third day: "David, how was your day? Anything exciting?"

"No . . ."

On the fourth day David looked at his mother and said gently but firmly, "Mom, I *am* going to say something. It's the same every day. If anything changes, I'll let you know."

As Sarah often says, she wishes she could have learned this in the fifth grade—David's fifth grade. She did cut down the twenty questions routine but would still try, from time to time, to draw out our son and get him to talk—to little avail.

She would say to me now and then, "I just don't understand David. He won't talk to me like I want him to talk." At that time we had not clearly zeroed in on how male and female children talk with parents. For example, females generally talk about their feelings more frequently than most males, including such topics as how they felt about their day. From my observations this behavior starts very young. Sons typically do not remember play-by-play conversations and experiences and eagerly share them as often as daughters do. It was perfectly normal for Sarah to ask, "How was your day?" and it was perfectly normal for David not to want to talk about it. (For more on this and other gender differences in children, see chapter 11: "Parenting Pink and Blue.")

*The Bible recognizes the unique struggles of youth: "He was afraid—he was still just a boy" (Judges 8:20 MSG).*

Later, when David was older and we were teaching Love & Respect principles in marriage conferences, Sarah found that a key to bonding with your son is not to confront him with direct questions but just to be with him, doing some activity he enjoys, "shoulder to shoulder."

# What Does It Mean to "Understand" Your Son or Daughter?

Gender differences in boys and girls were just one of many things Sarah and I learned on the job as we sought to understand our kids. Being aware of gender differences is helpful, but it is only part of a broader definition:

> To understand your child is to know and empathize with his developmental stages.

An obvious fact that parents often overlook is that their children—no matter what their age—are undeveloped and immature. Simply put, they need to grow up. After all, they are not grown-ups. For this reason we must recognize that a child—from toddler to teenager—will, as the Bible clearly states, "speak like a child, think like a child, reason like a child" and naturally enough, do "childish things" (1 Corinthians 13:11).

My mom would often recall a conversation she had with me when I was in first grade, which illustrates childlike reasoning. She asked me, "When your teacher gives you your spelling words from her list, does she skip around?" In all seriousness I responded, "No. She just stands there."

Children think literally first. They are kids and their comments and antics can bring a smile to every parent's face. The famous TV personality Art Linkletter said it best: "Kids say the darndest things!" Indeed they do, and we need to record "these things" in our memories for future retelling and sharing.

However, childishness can turn frustrating when our children do things that irritate us, and then we frustrate them when we grow impatient. At these moments we need to remember: childish means "immature, irresponsible, and silly." We need to ask ourselves, "What am I expecting? Will not my child act in childish ways?" Though such behavior upsets and exhausts us, and even feels disrespectful at times, our child or teenager means no ill will. We need to develop a spirit of understanding comparable to the spirit of generosity we discussed in the last chapter. Otherwise, we can seriously misunderstand our kids and the Family Crazy Cycle is sure to start spinning as we provoke them unnecessarily.

Ephesians 6:4 warns: "Fathers, do not provoke your children to anger," and Colossians 3:21 cautions: "Fathers, do not exasperate your children, so that they will not lose heart." I believe Paul is challenging fathers in particular in these verses because they can overdo correcting and appear too demanding. However, while mothers are typically more understanding than fathers, this warning from Scripture is for them as well.[1]

> *Be understanding.*
> *Love one another*
> *like members of*
> *the same family.*
>
> *—1 Peter 3:8 NIRV*

The first step in understanding your children is realizing how much they need to feel loved. Sounds simple? Be very aware, mom and dad, just because you possess deep love in your heart for your child does not mean you will automatically display a spirit of understanding or a willingness to understand. If there is too little understanding, a child can feel misunderstood, unaccepted, and unloved. This is why I do not think we dare take passages like Ephesians 6:4 and Colossians 3:21 too lightly.

But . . . living out these two passages is much easier said than done. Ironically, parents who are supposed to be more emotionally mature than their children are often guilty of being just the opposite. Put it this way: if I am regularly provoking my children to anger or exasperating them so they lose heart, I am not parenting in a mature way. True maturity seeks to serve the other person, not vice versa. Too many parents think parenting is a matter of getting their kids to understand what they—the parents—want, and then to do it respectfully. Sarah and I learned, often the hard way, that it is just the opposite: you get children to be obedient and respectful by loving them and understanding them. At times this may seem impossible, but it does work in the long run.

Remember that the critical question is always this:

> How do I understand my children so
> they feel loved and are also motivated
> to act respectfully toward me?

## How to Provoke Your Kids Without Really Trying

Think with me about how we adults can cross the line and frustrate our kids. When God's Word tells us not to provoke them in anger or exasperate them (Ephesians 6:4; Colossians 3:21), it is understood that we should know where that line is. Here are just some ways we can cross the line—more easily than we might think.

*Being too aggressive or physical* can easily cross the line. I am not saying you never discipline your children or take them in hand (see chapter 7: "Discipline"). I am talking about losing your patience or your cool and being too strong with the child, verbally or physically. It is easy to raise your voice to get them to listen; to grab them firmly and jerk them around while trying to get them to obey. Some children have to put up with much worse. I have many letters from parents telling of how they were abused as children, and I know from my personal experience as a child, the fear, frustration, and anger as I watched my father verbally abuse my mother. But whatever the level, harsh language and rough treatment provoke and anger any child, and eventually the child will close off to the parent.

*Breaking promises* can cross the line, even when mom and dad believe there is a good excuse for not showing up or following through on what was promised. One of the worst scenarios is the child who is left waiting for a parent who never returns. A friend of mine vividly recalls seeing his mother drive away after promising she would return in two weeks. For months he watched from the window, his heart leaping with hope when a blue car like hers went by. He recalls: "It would have been better to hear, 'I am an alcoholic and won't be coming back, but Grandma will care for you.'" Instead his eight-year-old heart was broken by her broken promise.

But any broken promise—failing to attend your child's program or game, not bringing a toy after a business trip—no matter how minor it might seem to you, can anger and exasperate your child. The point is clear: keep your promises to your children at all costs. As Scripture puts it, "Broken promises are worse than rain clouds that don't bring rain" (Proverbs 25:14 CEV).

When you simply cannot keep a promise, due to circumstances beyond your control, ask forgiveness and arrange for a makeup whenever possible. Following is an e-mail I found in my archives, which I had written to Joy, then age eleven, after I had to break a date we had planned together:

Dear Pinky,

My schedule was filled up this afternoon from 3:00 to 5:00. But this will work out better. Mom and I decided that on Monday, since you don't have school, we could do three things: 1. Go to the athletic club. 2. Go out to lunch. 3. Go shopping. I apologize for causing you to wait several more days. At 11, that can be frustrating. Yet we definitely have something to look forward to.

Joy tells me she does not remember how she responded to my note, but the important thing is that it did make her feel a little better. Any note or spoken word of apology will let children know you are aware of what you did and their feelings do matter.

*Name-calling* crosses the line more often than not, even when done as kidding—"just for fun." And if you call your child a name when irritated or angry, it is sure to do damage. My dad's term of *useless*, which he used on me on different occasions, was another reason I shut off my spirit from him for many years. I know if Dad were alive today, he would apologize. I believe in his deepest heart he did not want to react this way, yet his reactions deflated me.

I say again: *never* call your children names, or you will lose their hearts. I am surprised by the emotions that well up within me as I write this. Name-calling in the family is *not* a good thing. Truly, the tongue can be a "fire, the very world of iniquity" (James 3:6).

*False or hasty accusations without fully checking and listening* can be particularly harmful. When Joy was a teenager, I walked in while she and her boyfriend were wrestling on the floor in our living room, all in fun, but it brought up all kinds of red flags for me. I called her aside in private (at least I had the sense to do that) and tried to explain how this kind of close contact can arouse a young man. Joy was stunned and mortified. For her and her boyfriend, it was strictly innocent and playful, and all she could hear was that I was blaming her for something that just was not happening. Joy erupted in angry tears, and she was closed off to me for no short amount of time.

Was I wrong for confronting my daughter? That may be arguable (I was just trying to be a helpful father), but what is not up for debate is that I could have handled it differently. I could have stepped back and asked myself: "How will Joy feel if I say something right now? Should I let it go? What would Sarah counsel?" Sarah later told me I had blown it big-time, and she had to run a lot of interference for me to help Joy forgive me.

To further illustrate the impact this incident had on Joy, when I asked my grown children to give me examples of how I had blown it over the years, she quickly remembered the wrestling match lecture. I was mortified a second time and again felt all kinds of doubts about having any right to address a topic such as parenting. Fortunately, today Joy and I have a completely open daughter-dad friendship. When I shared my guilty and heavy heart over how I had hurt her, she said, "Dad, don't fail to see all the things you did right. Besides, if you are going to help parents accept God's grace, you need to accept His grace and my forgiveness as well."

False or hasty accusations can be especially harmful to teenagers because they are in the midst of trying to understand themselves and become independent. But falsely accusing your children at any age, without getting all the facts, is a surefire way to exasperate and anger them. Scripture puts it well: "Take note of this: Everyone should be quick to listen, slow to speak" (James 1:19 NIV). In other words, listen attentively and learn the facts before talking or acting. Proverbs 18:13 wisely counsels: "Answering before listening is both stupid and rude" (MSG).

Because I had included a big section on "listening attentively and caringly" in my PhD dissertation on the family, I thought I knew the basics, but my kids taught me a lot more than my grad school studies ever did.

For example, listening correctly usually means looking directly into their eyes. At ages three and four, Joy would grab my face and turn it toward her, saying, "Daddy, look at me." When my boys would catch me looking away when they were trying to tell me something, they were more apt to say, "You aren't even listening. You don't care about what I'm saying." I might have thought I was listening, but my kids were my best teachers at letting me know when I blew it.

David tells me now that as a young boy he felt I was always attempting to explain why I was telling him whatever it was I wanted him to understand. He knew I wanted to understand him, but he rarely felt that I did. This is one of my "losses" that pains me. Both Sarah and I feel we made a huge mistake in this area. We tended to react rather than respond. We tended to presume we knew rather than make sure we knew. We tended to give quick answers rather than say, "Let me think about that for a while."

Listening is an art, and even today I am still learning. One thing I have learned: parenting is not about getting your children to understand your instructions, advice, or guidance as much as it is about trying to understand them—how they feel and what they are trying to tell you.

Perhaps you can learn from what I share of our mistakes. What your children need and long for is that you seek to understand them, and there is no better way to start than to listen.

*Unreasonable expectations, requests, or demands* are another over-the-line mistake parents can easily make because they just are not aware their children are not capable of what they ask.

Sometimes parents do not see things through their children's eyes because they are too busy trying to live their lives through them. A father coaches his daughter's soccer team and because she is his best player, he pushes her relentlessly to perform. Although he claims he is doing it for her good, he really wants to fulfill only his own need for significance. The girl grows tired of the constant pressure and eventually refuses to play, which causes the father to erupt in anger for what he sees as her disrespect. She closes off in anger and loss of heart.

Many spins on the Family Crazy Cycle can be traced back to expecting more than our children can handle. When we push them beyond their maturation level, they can (and do) erupt in anger (Ephesians 6:4) or deflate in defeat (Colossians 3:21). A woman wrote about always wanting to be "Daddy's little girl, but no matter how hard I tried to be perfect, he never once said he was proud of me or just hugged me . . . no matter what I did it would never be good enough for him. Eventually I pretended that it didn't matter. I isolated myself from him."

There are many ways to cross the line and exasperate your child. A good principle to follow is to weigh your words or actions with questions like these:

"Will what I am about to say sound loving to my child?"

"Am I trying to see things through this little person's eyes?"

"Can I remember how it was when I was a teenager?"

Just stopping to ask yourself one of these questions is a good start, but there is still more to learn about exasperation; and for most parents, one more very big question must be answered.

# How Easily Do You "Give Away Your Keys"?

Being emotionally mature and not doing things to provoke and exasperate our kids is one challenge, but what about those times when they provoke and exasperate *us*? In the heat of the battle, we must remain calm and collected. As Proverbs 17:27 puts it, "He who restrains his words has knowledge, and he who has a cool spirit is a man of understanding."

It is our job to be emotionally in control, never verbally cruel. We must be able to take it. We are the grown-ups. We are driving the car, so to speak, and we must not give away the keys by indulging in our own form of childish behavior.

How easily can your children provoke and exasperate you? Here are some questions to think about.

*Do I tend to presume or prejudge?* In other words, do you read too much into it when your child disobeys, is late, or misbehaves in any of a dozen other ways each day? Do you suspect he sits up in his room late at night doing story boards on ways to make your blood boil?

Many parents get exasperated by predicting how their child will be disrespectful in certain situations. A mother foretells: "I knew she'd ignore my instructions on getting started with her homework. She does this to irritate me. I am wearing thin from her disrespectful disregard."

Parents exclaim: "If our children really respected us, they would listen! Of course we get angry. Isn't it right to be upset?" In many instances, the short answer is no—you are jumping to conclusions about your child's very normal behavior. You should deal with it but not

*In the family especially, "Through insolence comes nothing but strife" (Proverbs 13:10).*

in exasperation or anger. And do not always expect the worst from them.

*How patient am I . . . really?* This is the other side of the expectations coin. We expect our kids will act grown-up, not frustrate us, always be cooperative, and on and on. When they are not, we lose patience and zing them out of our own exasperation with, "Quit whining! Will you ever grow up?" Or that old standby: "Why can't you be like your older sister?" (or whomever). And, of course, from exasperation it is a short jump to off-the-charts anger.

When David was eleven or twelve, I pushed him up against the wall for lipping off about something, which was the climax to my frustration with him over his belligerence all Saturday morning. It was a forearm shiver that did not hurt him but got his attention. But I overreacted and was in the wrong. I lost my cool. I had never done such a thing before, nor did I do such a thing afterward, and I knew this was *my* issue. I felt horrible. I told him I was sorry and asked him to forgive me.

Interestingly, I asked David if he remembered my parenting failure. He replied, "No, I don't remember you pushing me against a wall. I remember another time when you picked me up to take me to the basement, and on the way down I grabbed the big, tall wooden shelf positioned against the wall and pulled it down. I'm still proud of that." I laughed and thanked the Lord for causing him to remember his bravado while forgetting my loss of control.

That scene of my impatience and anger is still with me. I had demonstrated greater immaturity than David did since, after all, I was the adult and he was the child. In my exasperation, I "gave away the keys."

*Do I unconsciously make my children responsible for my emotional well-being and happiness?* Does my self-image rise or fall based on my their conduct? When they are "good," do I feel good about myself? When they are "bad," do I feel bad about myself? I have counseled with many mothers who admit that in subtle ways they have made their children responsible for their sense of self-worth. This often leads to one of two bad results: these mothers give in to the demands of their children to get them to behave well, or they harbor resentment toward their children for "making" them feel bad about themselves for their lousy parenting.

I pray that you will not fall into this trap, but if you believe you might be there, you can escape. Your sense of self-worth as a parent should come not from your kids but from knowing the worth that Christ places on you. Children can affect us emotionally, but they must never be able to determine our self-image, which should depend on a healthy relationship with God. (For much more on this truth see chapter 13.)

*Am I too busy for my kids?* Some parents are so caught up in their adult world of goals, to-do lists, phone calls to make, e-mails to answer, constant texting, and on and on that they get exasperated when their kids want some of their time. Years ago I heard a speaker who told the story of a father busily working against a deadline behind closed doors in his home office. He begins to hear his three-year-old kicking the door ever so slightly. He tries to ignore the noise, but finally says sharply, "Jason, get away from the door! Daddy is trying to work."

All is quiet for a few seconds; then the father hears soft crying.

*Is this not how too many kids feel? "We wanted to skip rope, and you were always too tired; we wanted to talk, but you were always too busy" (Matthew 11:17 MSG).*

He opens the door and finds Jason on the floor, whimpering. "What did you want?" Dad asks. With lip quivering his little one stammers: "I just . . . want to . . . say, I . . . wuv . . . you."

The great philosopher Socrates said: "Beware of the barrenness of a busy life." When you are so busy that the slightest interruption exasperates you, it may easily lead to making your precious children feel unloved and misunderstood.

## Empathize . . . Then Do What Seems Best

Earlier in this chapter I defined understanding your children as the ability to know and empathize with them at whatever stage they might be in. By *empathize* I mean going beyond a simple statement that says, "That's too bad." Empathizing with someone means to understand and share another's feelings or thoughts, especially when that person is hurt or sad. You try to put yourself in the other person's shoes, and in this case the shoes are worn by your preschooler, your grade-schooler, or your teenager. You can empathize with your child because you can remember how it was to be new, to be different, to get a poor grade, to lose the game, or whatever it is your child is currently going through.

Granted, to empathize correctly is not always easy. Parenting well means showing enough empathy but not overdoing it either. Too much empathy can validate and feed a child's misplaced feelings of anger and self-pity. At its worst we can be so empathic that we rationalize and make excuses for poor behavior that can someday grow into habitual manipulation and even lying to us.

It is not an easy call. Again, we are found having to trust Abba Father as we do what seems best (Hebrews 12:10). Frequently a saving grace for Sarah and me was just trusting God. I know that sounds simplistic, but so often that is what Sarah and I fell back on (and still do). Instinctively, as Christ-following parents, we knew our deepest incentive to understand our children was based on our heavenly Father's understanding of us as His children. In fact, Jesus teaches that the heavenly Father feels about us the way we feel about our children (Matthew 7:7–11). Because of the Father's love for us, Sarah and I felt compelled to treat our kids the way He treated us. When we failed, we did so because we took our eyes off this truth.

As the Lord empathizes with our struggles, so we must empathize with our children's struggles. Hebrews 4:15 is our guide: "For we do not have a high priest who is unable to empathize with our weaknesses, but we have one who has been tempted in every way, just as we are—yet he did not sin" (NIV[2]).

What if we fail to understand and empathize?

When you blow it, seek forgiveness. In *Love & Respect* I said the most powerful words in any marriage are: "I'm sorry. Will you please forgive me?" The same seven words apply to parenting. When we fail to understand, when we step over that line and exasperate them, we can say things like these:

> "I am sorry. I got angry and wasn't thinking straight. I was wrong. Will you please forgive me?"

> "I spoke before I knew the whole story. I blew it. I apologize."

However you want to say it, be assured that your children understand "Will you forgive me?" when it comes from a sorrowful parent. And if you seldom say it, they will notice that too. Sarah commented: "Saying 'I was wrong; please forgive me' has always been important to me as a parent. I can remember my mother admitting she was wrong only twice. I loved my mother dearly, but I just longed to hear her say, 'I am sorry' because I knew there were times when she was wrong."

Bottom line: our children feel accepted and loved when we apologize for crossing the line . . . and that is always a good start toward understanding.

———

For more information on the following topics, go to
www.loveandrespect.com/parent/understanding:

- How Joseph and Mary approached twelve-year-old Jesus with understanding
- The long-term effects of empathizing and not empathizing
- Are there limits to understanding?
- How much should we lean on our own understanding?

# Lifestyles of the Eggerichs Family

(as told through the eyes of the youngest child, Joy)

My father, near the end of his time at military school. He was about to be introduced to college life and something he had been missing for the past five years . . . the opposite sex.

My parents, in youthful bliss, having no clue how their lives would change when their three cherubs would enter the world. Enjoy your cake, Mom and Dad. We're coming!

My dad's family was either grafting my mother into the Eggerichs family or trying to become the Partridge family.

My young parents with my oldest brother, Jonathan. The calm before the storm (as well as color in their wardrobe before they went black).

Pretty pumped red-footed PJs still come in preteen sizes.

For almost twenty years my dad preached at East Lansing Trinity Church. In 1982, my entrance into the world increased church attendance by one.

Before the days of smartphone camera redos.

And then the camera
was beaned.

And David told me
I was annoying.

I actually have no
sarcastic comment
to make. I think
this might be
one of the cutest
kid photos ever.

Wait
a
second!

Moments later the spoon may or may not have gone into my eye . . . typical meal time.

For a few years of our childhood, Mom took on the task of homeschooling us. Some first-day-of-school photos on the front step ended with us turning around and walking back inside. Slightly anticlimactic, but Mom was a champ for giving it a go!

I don't think any of us were happy about this.

My dad was great, but sometimes his face just said, "Take me far, far away from the noise."

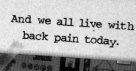
And we all live with
back pain today.

Aside from Jonathan looking
slightly frightened, this photo
may lead you to believe we
were normal. Don't be fooled!

And seconds
later we had
scrambled eggs.

Family nativity play:
the only time when
being married to your
brother and having
your other brother
bow to you are okay.

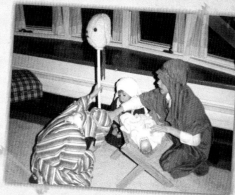

I think we ate at this table
until we left for college.

We found a red stool in
the woods and snapped
a candid photo.

Typical Friday
night of war
paint and belly–
button grabs.

Probably the one
time we all did the
dishes together. And
hopefully the last
time my dad wore
a fitted shirt.

I wonder if there will come a time when families stop coordinating their clothing with the holiday decorations. Thankfully, the passing of the '80s hairstyles will prevent grandfathers from getting lost in family photos.

Coffee helps many parents survive this stage.

My parents never put us in any dangerous, non-child-appropriate situations.

There is so much I want to say about my brothers' shirts, my mom's eye makeup, and my dress—with—bib stage . . . but I won't.

The era in which my brothers were thrilled to take family photos and my parents were subconsciously trying to get me to early enroll for the navy.

My brothers during their maybe-I'll-get-discovered phase.

Apparently my father was the only one who made it to the tanning beds before this family photo.

And look! We all survived!
(L to R: Jonathan, Sarah, Jackson, being held by Emerson, Sarah, David, and Joy)

# 6

## INSTRUCT

### *Not Too Much . . . but Just Enough "Stuff Like That"*

To love your children using G-U-I-D-E-S:

When I pastored many years ago, a young man wrote to tell me of how he grew up in a home in the 1960s that was at the end of a long private drive. People often drove down there just to snoop, or sometimes younger couples would park. The turnaround area was small, and drivers often would swing into the yard, spinning their tires and leaving ruts in the lawn. One day he and his father were out fixing ruts (again), and he said disgustedly, "Man, couldn't you just bash those guys?"

His father just shrugged and said, "No, not really."

When he asked why, his dad answered, "There are a lot more important things than grass."

He did not understand what his dad meant and pushed the matter further: "Like what?"

His dad answered with eight words that made a powerful impact on his life: "Like kindness, brotherhood, love . . . and stuff like that."

The young man, writing years later, closed his letter: "I suppose this sounds like a funny story, but it has made a lasting impression on me. This teaching moment has put a lot of things into perspective for me. Furthermore, my father made it clear that he loved me . . . but his modeling of his righteous walk with Christ . . . was most important."

When he uttered those words that stuck with his son for life, I doubt this father thought to himself, *Oh, here is a great teachable opportunity to impart wisdom to my son.* Most likely he was not thinking of Ephesians 6:4, which says, "Bring them up in the . . . instruction of the Lord," but he was living it, and that is the best kind of teaching a parent can do. Children pay attention when they ask why and receive insights from a humble parent's heart.

> *As for God's commands, "You shall teach them diligently to your sons and shall talk of them when you sit in your house and when you walk by the way and when you lie down and when you rise up"* (Deuteronomy 6:7).

Such moments with our children reveal what we truly believe. Today we live in a world of incredible temptation and growing cynicism toward the things of Christ. If we are the "real deal" as godly parents, we will stand head and shoulders above all other influences as we seek to teach our kids "kindness, brotherhood, love . . . and stuff like that."

## You Are Your Child's Most Important Teacher

No one is more important than parents when it comes to imparting truth to children. As Proverbs 1:8 puts it: "Listen, my son, to your father's instruction and do not forsake your mother's teaching" (NIV). But after being in ministry a long time I know that many believers are not completely convinced they are the most important teachers their children have. After all, well-trained people teach their kids—at school, at church, on the athletic field or court. It is tempting to think, *I can count on others to instruct my kids better than I can. My job is to care for them, earn a living, love them, support them . . . isn't that important?*

All that is very important, but it is not enough. More is needed, and that is why parents are commanded to bring up their children in the "instruction of the Lord." The Greek word for *instruction* in Ephesians 6:4 relates to what is spoken to the child as a teaching, warning, or encouragement. According to Paul, this verbal instruction should come from the inspired writings of the Bible. When Paul wrote to Timothy, he told the young pastor, "From childhood you have known the sacred writings which are able to give you the wisdom that leads to salvation through faith which is in Christ Jesus. All Scripture is inspired by God and profitable for teaching, for reproof, for correction, for training in righteousness" (2 Timothy 3:15–16).

Paul was referring in part to the Old Testament writings, which were imparted to Timothy by his mother, Eunice, and grandmother Lois, but he was also thinking of the words and ways of Jesus, who Himself said, "It is written, 'Man shall not live on bread alone, but on every word that proceeds out of the mouth of God'" (Matthew 4:4). As Christ followers we believe in a revelatory worldview, that Abba is there and that He has spoken to us primarily through His Son. This is why Paul wrote in Romans 10:17, "So faith comes from hearing, and hearing by the word of Christ." When we keep Christ central in our hearts, we will not stray from bringing up our children in the instruction of the Lord Jesus. We will bring the heart of our child to the heart of Christ.[1]

# What Should We Teach?

I believe our teaching involves two major areas.

First, we anchor our kids in God's saving truths. What a privilege to look for ways to share the plan of salvation with our children. If we do not know how to lead them to Christ, those who work with children in the church can provide numerous tools to show us how. There is no greater joy than to lead our very own children to Christ. But whether we explain the gospel message to them or someone at church does, there is nothing—absolutely nothing—more important for eternity. What good is it if we teach our children how to succeed in the world while they forfeit their souls (Matthew 16:26)?

When my mom came to Christ at age fifty-three, she held up a Bible in front of me with tears running down her cheeks as she said, "All my life it was right here, and no one ever told me about a personal relationship with Christ." Mom is in heaven, but I know she would say to all parents, "Instruct your children in the sacred writings to give them wisdom 'that leads to salvation through faith which is in Christ Jesus' (2 Timothy 3:15). Don't let them go fifty-three years not knowing!" (See chapter 9: "Supplicate," about my daughter, Joy, coming to Christ at age five.)

Second, train them in how to behave wisely in daily living. Solomon began the book of Proverbs with these teachings: "for gaining wisdom and instruction; for understanding words of insight; for receiving instruction in prudent behavior, doing what is right and just and fair" (Proverbs 1:2–3 NIV).

Solomon's words suggest many specific character qualities and competencies. When we instruct our kids on various topics, we must get at the *why*, explaining the reasons behind the teaching. For example, we do not lie, cheat, or steal not only because doing so is wrong but also because it hurts the heart of God, who loves us; undermines our relationships with others; and harms our reputation. I used to say to the kids, "When God says no, He is saying, 'Don't hurt yourself.'" What seems right at the moment, in the long run, can lead to death (Proverbs 14:12). We might ask our kids, "Do you know what the last words of an idiot behind the wheel are? 'Watch this!'"

"But Emerson, I feel so inadequate to instruct my kids from the Bible. I have no Bible training—no degree in biblical ethics and morality and all the other things that can come up. My kids are full of endless questions." I understand. My kids had (and still seem to have) endless questions, and all the degrees I earned did not always help. (Actually, it has often occurred to me that I am educated beyond my intelligence.)

Nonetheless, there are several things every parent can do when it comes to bringing up the children in the "instruction of the Lord" (Ephesians 6:4).

## Let the Word of Christ Dwell in You Richly

There is nothing in the Bible about parents being seminary trained in order to teach their children. A poor, uneducated mother in an African tribe can instruct her children in the things of Christ. She may not be able to read, but as she hears the words of Christ preached and lets those words take up residence within her soul, she becomes the best conduit in God's eyes for instructing her children.

When the apostle Paul instructed parents in Colossians 3:21, "Fathers, do not exasperate your children, so that they will not lose heart," he was following up on what he said in verses 16 and

17, about letting "the word of Christ richly dwell within you." He is telling parents that when Christ's words fill their hearts, they become natural conduits for the "instruction of the Lord" Jesus (Ephesians 6:4). I have observed that when parents enjoy the Lord and meditate on His truth, it spills out as they communicate with their kids. I say to all parents: "Never, ever think that you are ill prepared to instruct your children when the words of Christ are living in you. You are Christ's favorite professor. This is the Lord's primary means of implanting His instruction in your kids. Stand tall! You are Christ's vessel!" (For ideas for what to say to your children as you teach them about love and respect, see Appendix A: Love & Respect Goals for Our Family.)

There are also godly, wise teachers who can help reinforce our parental instruction. Do not hesitate to utilize the local church, Christian camps, and schools to bolster what you teach at home. The church can make a huge impression through its many programs that focus on biblical child development. Furthermore, the church can offer godly support for you as a parent, as you fellowship and study with like-minded believers.

## Live What You Teach

As we saw in the story of the dad and his son repairing the lawn, the power of example is incalculable. As one parent told me, "I see in my own children that my instructing is useless unless I model what I tell them."

The beautiful thing is that almost daily something arises that allows us to teach our kids what we believe and why we believe it. Look for these challenges as teachable moments that allow you to reveal your heart to the heart of your child. For instance, a grade-schooler struggles with his homework and finally asks his mother if she would do it for him. She objects, "It wouldn't be right."

"But Mom," pleads the boy. "You could at least *try*!"

Mom might suppress a smile, but she should let her son know that honesty is better than cheating every time. He does not like it when his friends cheat at games, and his teacher does not like it when her students cheat against her and, more importantly, against themselves.

Truly, with our children what we believe is caught more than taught. After the church service a little boy tells the pastor, "When I grow up, I'm going to give you some money."

"Well, thank you," the pastor replies. "But why?"

"Because my daddy says you're one of the poorest preachers we've ever had."[2]

Take care what you do and say. Your children are watching and listening, and often they take you quite literally.

## Fill the Teachable Moments with What Seems Best

On the edge of divorce, Steve and Jackie came to a Love & Respect Weekend as a "last-ditch effort" to save their marriage. They made some progress and later, back home, their five-year-old son watched the Love & Respect marriage videos along with them as they worked to put their marriage back together. As this couple continued to heal, Jackie e-mailed me: "I was in the car with my son, and I must have audibly sighed without realizing it. Matthew said to me, 'Mommy, if you're feeling blue, you need to do what Sarah said on the video and be thankful!' I told him he was right, and we talked about all the things we could be thankful for that day."

Talk about teachable moments! And in this case, a five-year-old brought the teaching full circle.

Sometimes teaching moments can be unpleasant and it takes courage to confront your child with truth, lovingly and respectfully spoken. When my son David was fourteen, I came upon him while he was playing baseball on his computer. I could see he was frustrated and asked, "What happened? Did you strike out?" Angrily, David shoved me away. The shove was more symbolic of his frustration than a show of anger toward me, but I was still shocked. David had never shoved me like that before (and he never did again). I said nothing, but a little later I wrote him a note about what had happened:

*As parents let us hear this scripture: "The tongue of the wise makes knowledge acceptable" (Proverbs 15:2).*

Dear David,

Sometimes things happen very quickly, catching us off guard . . . when we are angry, we can act impulsively. We can let our emotions, rather than our hearts and minds, control us. Is it possible at times like that to say, "I am feeling frustrated and angry right now. I'd like to put my foot through this screen"? I am confident we can say things like this. We can say in words what we are feeling without letting those feelings explode into such things as pushing another person.

That incident served as a teaching moment when I tried to do what seemed best for David. You may or may not feel comfortable with writing your children notes. But what is important is to take advantage of those teachable moments, doing as Hebrews 12:10 describes and teaching your children as you think best. (For more on this see chapter 7: "**D**iscipline.")

## A Word About Teaching "Respect 101"

As we seek to learn to be loving parents, our kids need to learn to be respectful children. A father wrote: "I have started working very closely with my sons (ten and twelve), teaching them to treat each other with respect and kindness regardless if they perceive that the other does not 'deserve it' . . . and that they are to be respectful to Mom, no matter what. NO EXCEPTIONS."

He went on to say, "Instead of my usually telling them to 'knock it off' when they are quarreling, I stop them and ask each individually if his own behavior was respectful. Amazingly, one will say, 'No, it wasn't,' and sometimes even apologize to the other without prompting. While they still fight (as brothers do), they do not fight the same. I catch them saying things like, 'What you said did not feel very nice—what did I do?' and 'Dad, I think I hurt Mommy's feelings—what did I do?'"

*There are moments when as parents we appeal, "My child, remember my teachings and instructions and obey them completely" (Proverbs 3:1 CEV).*

"What did I do?" is a perfect lead-in for a teachable moment. Guide the child in thinking back to what happened and what was said as you help him recognize what was not respectful and how to avoid it next time (also see appendix A).

# What About Too Much or Too Little Instruction?

As for too much instruction, I made this mistake. Not that I stuffed the Bible down their throats daily, but in unison my kids tell me today that I overdid it by writing treatises on various issues that seemed to me to be mini-crises in their lives. My lectures on paper shamed them more than enlightened them. Though they agree that I tried to be fair and balanced and have empathy, they felt that I overloaded them with information and it did not make the inroads into their hearts that I could have made had I listened more and lectured less.

But what of the other side of the instruction coin—too little information because parents fail to give clear and fair instruction on even the simplest matters of daily living? Does your child sometimes (maybe often) say, "You didn't tell me that! It's not my fault!"? One mother commented, "I have this issue with Mark and he is usually right . . . he is our third child, and I forget which kid I have told what."

I know how Mark feels because it happened to me when I was small. I loved my dad, but he had trouble communicating with me, especially if I tried to help him with projects around the house.

One frequent project was fixing the pump motor on the swimming pool filter that was always running because my mother taught swimming classes. My dad would lie under the pump, like a mechanic under a car, and sometimes call to me to go get him "an Allen wrench" or a "monkey wrench." He never showed me what either of the wrenches looked like; he just would talk fast while I stood there, getting nervous about not being able to find the wrench or do what he asked. I would go and try my eight-year-old best to find what he wanted and often returned empty-handed, or sometimes I would just say, "I don't know what that is."

Sighing and grumbling, my dad would slide out from under the pump, and as he got up to go get what he needed, say, "You're as useless as !@#$% on a boar." For years I thought he said "board." I had no idea what he meant, but I did hear the word *useless*. Totally mortified and exasperated, I would just go away, feeling not only useless but as though I was a huge disappointment to my dad.

By contrast, a mother wrote,

When Matthew, our oldest son, was three, it was repair time for the lawn mower. As he watched my husband work, there was a need for a screwdriver. Allen explained to our son the differences in screwdrivers. Matthew went off to the box and returned with the tool! Allen thanked him, to which he replied, "Hey Dad, you need me!" I learned from my husband to always include the children in our activities. It takes time when they're younger, and it usually takes longer than normal at first and is usually much messier, too, but their self-esteem, sense of belonging, and being respected and loved is worth it all.

This father's loving patience also underscores the importance of instructing with the right tone of voice and manner. If you sound and look as though you think your child is brain-dead, your child will feel unloved and stupid (and probably not learn very much). Instructing with hostility and contempt never works with any human being.

# The Teenage Brain Finally Does Develop

Though younger kids are teachable, they may not appear that way when they hit their teens. As a child, and especially in her teens, our daughter, Joy, did not sit at my feet and cry out, "Daddy, teach me! Teach me!" Yet, as she entered her midtwenties she woke from her adolescent trance and today appeals to me to mentor her. You may have heard Mark Twain's observation: "When I was a boy of fourteen, my father was so ignorant I could hardly stand to have the old man around. But when I got to be twenty-one, I was astonished at how much the old man had learned in seven years."[3]

Cutting-edge research in brain development[4] helps explain why teenagers can be so unreasonable, overdramatic, and irrational while appearing to think they know it all. It seems the brain makes huge leaps in development during adolescence as it becomes more interconnected and gains in processing power and decision-making skills. But despite its growth, the teenage brain still relies more on its emotional functions rather than the rational. This helps explain why they may "know better" but do stupid, dangerous things.

When Joy recently read an article on teenage brain development, she e-mailed me:

This resonated with me . . . it gives a little clarity to the roller coaster of emotions and irrational decisions the teen makes. It also creates empathy. I felt things *so* strongly in high school . . . the times you or Mom empathized with the drama I was experiencing made me want to open up more to you. Empathy will allow a feeling of safety for the kids . . . where parents can probably speak some rational thinking that might be received. "Might" is the operative word.

Teenage haughtiness and presumption usually subsides when they meet life head-on and simultaneously see "how much their parents have grown." Meanwhile, parents must try to stay cool and hang in there as they instruct.

## Continually Ask God for Help

Our last principle is probably the most important of all: pray without ceasing as you go about fulfilling God's call to bring your children up in the instruction of the Lord. This is a huge task, and I find comfort in knowing that He will help us obey what He commands us to do—if we ask.

We will talk more about prayer in chapter 9: "Supplicate," but when it comes to instructing our children, an effective prayer can be a simple "Lord, give me wisdom right now!" when we are struggling to respond in the moment. And, of course, a prayer as we begin each day of parenting is always wise.

## A Prayer for Guidance When Instructing

"Lord, give us wisdom to find the right balance when instructing our children: not 'too much' that turns them off and not 'too little' so they have no guidance. Help us live what we teach, allowing Your words to dwell in us richly. Give us insight and courage to use the teachable moments according to what seems best."

For more information on the following topics, go to
www.loveandrespect.com/parent/instruction:

- More on teaching respect 101
- How to be a parenting team when instructing
- How to avoid "over-instructing" your kids

# 7

## DISCIPLINE

### Confront . . . Correct . . . Comfort

To love your children using G-U-I-D-E-S:
When I was around nine or ten, I locked my mom and sister, Ann, out of the house.

I have long ago forgotten why. I do recall that they kept knocking and asking me to open the door, but I refused as I peered through the window at them. I was not happy about something, and neither were they at this point. Interestingly, as Mom gazed at me through the window, she did not scream at my disrespectful behavior. Instead, after she made several dignified requests for me to open the door, she turned around and walked to the car with my sister. They got in and drove off.

Thirty minutes later Mom and Ann returned. I watched her car come down the hill, but what I saw next took my breath away. A police car was following her right to our house! I broke out in a cold sweat. Mom must have lodged a complaint, and the policeman intended to jail me! By then I had unlocked the door, and as Mom walked by me, she nonchalantly said, "There is someone in the driveway who wants to talk to you." Mom did not rant and rave, screaming things like, "Boy, are you in trouble now!" She went into another room and expected me to go see our visitor. I did.

As I walked up to the state police car, chills went down my spine as I noticed a shotgun propped up on the dashboard. Then I saw a huge man with a "Smokey the Bear" hat on his head, seated behind the steering wheel. He got out of the car, and I stood there trembling, looking up and up. He was at least six foot five, and he may have even been closer to ten feet tall!

With a deep voice he asked, "Do you always lock your mommy and sister out of the house? What kind of a man are you? Is this something you plan on doing again? I am thinking that you are never going to do this again. Is that true? Want to see my shotgun?"

Sheepishly I said that I would never do it again, and yes, I wanted to see his shotgun. Somehow in that exchange, as we sat there looking at his shotgun, he made me feel as though I were a man and that men do not do this kind of thing.

I never locked my mom out of the house again. Real men don't do that.

*Just any kind of discipline misses the point. "Wise discipline imparts wisdom" (Proverbs 29:15 MSG).*

I share this little drama from my childhood to illustrate the obvious: children need discipline. Despite the Bible's clear command for children to honor their father and mother (Exodus 20:12), they do not always do so. In fact, they seem born to disobey (Romans 3:23; Galatians 3:22). Though we may tenderly love them by Giving, Understanding, and Instructing them, our tender love can fall short of motivating them to obey in every area.

*What do we do then?*

# Discipline Is *Not* Punishment

When it comes to our children, Ephesians 6:4 clearly commands parents to "bring them up in the discipline . . . of the Lord." The Greek word for "discipline" in Ephesians 6:4 is *paideia* and entails the idea of "correcting." We are to correct our kids for future good, not just point out past mistakes. Discipline involves helping a child amend, alter, and improve his choices and conduct. In that sense, we are training our child to do the right and righteous thing.

> *We yearn for our children to learn. Therefore "discipline your children while they are young enough to learn"* (Proverbs 19:18 GNT).

Although the reproof is to produce sorrow (*paideia* in Hebrews 12:5, 11), such discipline is *not* punishment. Discipline puts the child back on the right track. We must do our best to send a positive message of correction and point them to a better way, without a tone of "You will pay!"

Not all behavior that irritates a parent is wrongdoing. Kids are childish, immature, and destined to do many annoying things that are not disrespectful defiance. Part of our process is to discern the difference, to be sure that an incident is truly a cause for discipline.

David recalls that at age nine his passion was to become a major-league pitcher. He had seen something on TV about how he could take some tape and outline a strike zone on the back of our garage, which was made of aluminum siding. He did not consider that every pitch would leave an obvious cavity. In his mind nobody would mind the huge dents in the aluminum, and he threw about fifteen pitches. He recalls not getting into that much trouble because "you guys realized how important baseball was to me, and I innocently did what I did. Stupid? Yes, but not intentionally wrong."

As David and I reminisced about this incident, I told him, "I remember it well. I was so sad. I was devastated! I couldn't shake it for weeks. You threw only two strikes out of fifteen!"

Granted, it is not always easy to make the call on the spot as to what is disobedient and what is childish lack of judgment. In chapter 4, I introduced an important principle for parenting built upon the truth found in Hebrews 12:10, about fathers (and mothers): "For they disciplined us for a short time as seemed best to them." We see from this text that parenting God's way often leaves us with no absolute formulas, and we must make subjective judgment calls when disciplining. Even so, Sarah and I derived much comfort from Hebrews 12:10, knowing that it was okay to have these feelings of uncertainty as we weighed the pros and cons. We can have peace of mind, even though we hear no voice from heaven saying, "This is the way, walk in it" (Isaiah 30:21).

But let's be honest: disciplining our children is not fun—for them or us. We learn in Hebrews 12:11 that "all discipline for the moment seems not to be joyful, but sorrowful." It is not fun for children to be corrected or reprimanded, and it is often challenging, demanding, and worse for the weary parent who has to make the same correction for what seems to be the ten thousandth time. If discipline causes all this discomfort and unhappiness, why bother?

We learn the main answer from our heavenly Father: "THOSE WHOM THE LORD LOVES HE DISCIPLINES" (Hebrews 12:6; see also Proverbs 3:12). The writer of Hebrews went on to make this point: "For what son is there whom his father does not discipline?"

(Hebrews 12:7). By implication, then, a dad disciplines because he loves his child.

Bottom line: *we discipline because we care.*

## Our Plan for How We *Lovingly* Disciplined Our Children

When Sarah and I were raising our children and looking to the Bible for what it had to say about discipline, we did what we believed God called us to do, while leaving the results to Him. We tried to be as loving and fair as possible so that we would not crush their spirits. We tried to hear their hearts when addressing the discipline yet stay the course. Like all parents, Sarah and I regret many mistakes. Today our children tell us they struggled with guilt and shame as "the pastor's kids." Our attempts to discipline them with grace and forgiveness sometimes fell short. At the same time, we did some things right. Jonathan, our oldest and a Christian clinical psychologist, wrote at age thirty-six:

*Loving and wise discipline results in a child's respect: "We had earthly fathers to discipline us, and we respected them" (Hebrews 12:9).*

> My parents have influenced me tremendously on issues such as parenting, schooling, and faith. Things were a little different, I suppose, growing up in a pastor's home, in that everyone knew everything about us, but for the most part we lived a normal childhood with loving and kind parents. Today I value the wisdom and discernment that they displayed in parenting. Due

to their influence I believe that a parent should be an authority and influence in a child's life. Rules should be clear and openly discussed. Discipline should occur when necessary, but never in anger. I do not remember my parents disciplining us in anger. Did they get angry? Of course. But they always waited and made decisions as a team. When they did discipline us, we were told it was because they loved us. That is not an easy thing for a child to wrap his head around and many times I said, "Yeah right." But today I cherish their approach.

What was our approach? We tried to . . .

1. create rules that are clear and fair.
2. confront and correct without anger.
3. enact consequences when necessary.
4. reward obedience and reaffirm love no matter what.

We learned that below two years of age it is more helpful to distract the child rather than enact discipline, which is a bit beyond his understanding. For example, if the child is upset, it often works to say something like, "Oh, look at what the duck is doing in your book!" This may redirect the child's emotions and attention. But above two years children are usually not so easily distracted; you need simple rules and boundaries—in other words, discipline *as seems best.*

## Create Rules That Are Clear and Fair

"Creating rules" might sound legalistic, even totalitarian. However, in all of life there are rules. For example, we read in 2 Timothy 2:5:

"If anyone competes as an athlete, he does not win the prize unless he competes according to the rules." Games cannot be played without rules. Similarly, in the home we establish well-defined and reasonable rules that give direction and guide fair play among family members. Every rule we make for our kids should be clear and fair. And do not assume your children know the rules you have made. Instruction must precede discipline—always!

If we have no rules for our children, they will create rules for us. For example, if you allow the child to speak disrespectfully, you are letting the child make his own rule: "It is okay to use disrespectful speech." Rules are inevitable—yours or the kids'.

As you establish rules for your family, keep in mind that the basis of all good laws and rules is the golden rule: treat others as you want them to treat you. From the golden rule I devised what I call the "if-then" principle.

*The golden rule: "Treat others the same way you want them to treat you" (Luke 6:31).*

*If* you open something, *then* close it. *If* you turn something on, *then* turn it off. *If* you make a mess, *then* clean it up. *If* you unlock something, *then* lock it. For example, we can say to the child, "If someone unlocks the lock on your bike and does not relock it and it gets stolen, how will you feel?" The child knows he will be very upset, and he can easily see that if he unlocked his brother's bike and it got stolen, his brother would be upset as well. It is only fair that we treat others as we want them to treat us. The beautiful thing is that God designed us to live by the golden rule, and kids naturally understand it. (Dads need to still be reminded of it, though, as any mom can tell you. As Sarah and I worked on this chapter, she was quick to point out that just the day before I had left a cupboard door open and the lid off the peanut butter jar—again!)

I cannot overemphasize the need to tell your children the *why* behind any rule. Never try to bail out by simply saying, "Because I said so." This kind of iron-fisted approach is both intellectually lazy and unloving, and will just ignite more disciplinary problems. Rules should ring true to their hearts, not crush them.

We had two types of rules: nonnegotiable and negotiable.

## Nonnegotiable Rules Are Just That—Nonnegotiable

As Sarah and I settled into the task of parenting, we decided up front that no matter what the culture was saying, there are biblical rules that remain constant. "Always tell the truth" was one of our nonnegotiable rules, which we sought to teach as soon as our kids were old enough to begin to understand (roughly, around two). It is no coincidence that our nonnegotiable rules echo the Ten Commandments. And because nonnegotiable rules are based on divine law, they are "ageless and stageless." It made no difference how old our children were or what developmental stage they were going through. They learned daily that we do not lie, cheat, or steal. Why? *If* we are to be credible people, whom others love and respect, *then* we will not lie to, steal from, or cheat other people. No exceptions. And *why* should we not lie, cheat, or steal? As we don't want people to lie to us, cheat us, or steal from us, we must not do these things to them. The golden rule.

Another nonnegotiable rule in our home said: *If* we are to be individuals that other people want to be around, *then* we do not explode in anger and destroy things and hurt people. We taught that, as a family, we have zero tolerance for willfully breaking things and injuring others. Yes, we gave grace to our children when they were toddlers and threw occasional temper tantrums, but they soon learned that angry behavior was not acceptable and must absolutely cease. Besides, we don't want people to hurt us, so why would we hurt others? The golden rule.

Still another rule we took from the Ten Commandments was "We don't do things that hurt God's heart, but instead we always try to show our desire to trust and obey Him." For example, *if* we love God, *then* we do not take God's name in vain. Instead, we thank God for the good times as well as the less-than-good times. We seek to serve Him, not curse Him. And when we honor Him, He honors us. God applies the golden rule too.

Based on God's command, we created guidelines or rules to help our kids honor and respect us as their mother and father. We told them, "We expect respect. As we respect you, we expect your respect toward us. We aren't rude to you, so don't be rude to us. Fair is fair."

Even with nonnegotiable rules, we should show grace and forgiveness when our children fail, but we still hold the line. Showing grace never means we call that which is wrong an okay thing to do (Isaiah 5:20). Instead, we confess our wrongs and begin again because the nonnegotiable rules do not change, having stood the test of time.

## What Is a Negotiable Rule?

Negotiable rules are not etched in stone as the Ten Commandments were. They change as the child develops and moves through phases of growth and maturity. The negotiable rule is not ageless and stageless but very much revolves around the age and stage of the child.

Negotiable rules do not fit nicely into the if-then or golden rule classification. The best way to establish and enforce these rules is by saying, "This is best for you and all of us and for this reason." They go to bed at this time because they need the sleep. They eat the green beans because they need the nutrients. They call us to tell us where they are so we don't worry.

How many negotiable rules should a family have? Every family will be a bit different. We had rules dealing with curfew, bedtime hour, TV watching, wearing clean clothes, healthy eating, doing homework on time, fastening the seat belts, using our *inside* voices, and the list went on, according to what seemed necessary and fair. All of these were rooted in our desire to do what "seemed best" with a good reason.

For sure, we did not want too many rules, which would make us dictators who enacted a suffocating and pharisaical legalism with our "human" rules (Colossians 2:22 GNT). But neither did we wish to become indulgent parents who subscribed to an anti-rule position because we are free in Christ to such an extent that we ignore "the law of Christ" (1 Corinthians 9:21).

> A refusal to correct is a refusal to love; love your children by disciplining them.
>
> —*Proverbs 13:24* MSG

Sarah and I had our own rule that helped us with negotiating negotiable rules, which said, "Never change a rule or make an exception based on the child's emotional complaint." We strove never to send the message, "Complain loud enough and long enough, and the rule will be stretched or just plain overlooked."

Negotiable rules are, of course, negotiable, and occasional exceptions can be fun for all involved. ("Okay, you can stay up tonight and watch the gymnastic team compete at the Olympics.") Such times build memories. But when the exception to the rule becomes the rule, we have a problem. We are not creating a joyful child but a whining kid. Kids figure that out very quickly and conclude that if they irritate us incessantly, we will forgo the rule. Consistency is crucial. There can be no enforcing a rule one day ("Make your beds before breakfast") and letting it go the next ("Oh, that's okay. I'll make your bed; you're running late for school").

A good strategy is to be a "benevolent dictator" through most of their childhood years; then move to a more *democratic* approach as your kids enter teen years. Whenever possible and practical, let them help draft family rules. Your long-range goal is to move from control to counsel.

But what happens when they are unruly?

## Confront and Correct Without Anger

As we know, kids will not always follow the rules. Whatever your rules are, you will have to enforce them, meaning you must confront and correct your children when they break, ignore, or forget a rule. Parental discipline includes rebuke and correction and evidences love (Proverbs 13:1; 27:5).

When rules are disobeyed consciously or carelessly, it is vital that you confront and correct without anger or that condescending tone that suggests you think you are talking to idiots, which would only undermine what you are trying to do. How will your children learn to respect you if you angrily treat them without love? As

*God calls us to humbly and lovingly confront, and gives us examples of parents who failed: "His father had never crossed him at any time by asking, 'Why have you done so?'" (1 Kings 1:6).*

Scripture says, "A fool is quick-tempered, but a wise person stays calm when insulted" (Proverbs 12:16 NLT).

But what do we do when we are loving, the rule is fair, yet the child is disrespectful and disregards the rule? We confront, correct, and win—for the well-being of our child and the entire family. We must not be blind or deaf to habitual disrespect. The child needs to hear us say in a respectful tone, "You are being disrespectful and disobedient. You know the rule." Unfortunately, with some strong-willed children, to make rules simply invites their rebellion. Thus, God reveals to us to discipline, and in this type of situation we calmly say: "No good will come to you if you keep talking rudely. You need to decide right now to talk respectfully and apologize for your disrespect, or you'll receive the consequences" (more on consequences later in this chapter).

Children can learn that it is okay to protest a rule as long as they are respectful. We can inform them that they can get their point across to us more persuasively by being respectful even though they are upset. We can teach them, "You can learn to convey your feelings and opinions in a respectful way, and it will be much better for you if you do."

With very young children the best way to confront their disrespect is by giving them a "time-out." In a public setting when a child speaks disrespectfully, escort the child away from the situation in a calm and dignified manner. With the younger child get down on one knee and speak face-to-face about what happened. "You just called your sister stupid. That is disrespectful. Mom and Dad don't talk that way, and we won't allow you to talk that way. Do you understand?" Always assure the child, "If you are feeling frustrated by something, come to me and tell me how you feel. I will try to help you."

We must care enough to confront and correct. Indifference

is unloving. For example, a dad wrote about confronting his son who acted disrespectfully toward his mother: "I have changed my parenting approach to Sammy. While he was being rude to Karen in defying her instruction to practice the piano, I typically would not get involved. This time I took him into his room, and for the first time said, 'I cannot tolerate anyone using disrespectful words to your mamma, whether a neighbor, a friend, but especially not her son. It's your choice going forward.'" This dad awakened to the necessity of confronting rudeness, and it has worked.

As you consider how to apply any of these examples, keep in mind that "relationship most often determines response." By that I mean if we are always confronting but not nurturing the relationship, we are probably making more withdrawals than deposits and are emotionally bankrupting the relationship. On a positive note, a mother who sits for just ten minutes and watches her two boys play catch with a baseball (which energizes the boys in ways that mothers do not always understand) is making a big deposit in her relationship with them. Her corrections will be better received later, when she informs them that they must go to sleep and stop talking. A father who takes his daughter out for dinner, just the two of them, is making a deposit as well, and when he confronts her about cleaning up her room, she is likely to be more receptive. Generally speaking, your positive relationship with your child determines to a great degree your child's positive response to you (i.e., you show her love, and she will show you respect—the Family Energizing Cycle).

If we come down on our kids every time that they are unresponsive to this or that, we will frustrate them. Think about applying Proverbs 19:11 to your parenting style: "A person's wisdom yields patience; it is to one's glory to overlook an offense" (NIV).

At the same time, do not stuff all negative feelings. Our daughter reminded me that she remembers many times when Sarah and I got upset and showed it. "That resonated with me," she said. "Parents shouldn't be robots."

Yes, Sarah and I got angry plenty of times, but we always tried to live out Ephesians 4:26: "BE ANGRY AND yet DO NOT SIN; do not let the sun go down on your anger." Our credo read: "To control our children, we must first control ourselves. To discipline our children, we must be self-disciplined." Granted, some days were better than others, but as Proverbs 24:16 teaches, we kept getting back up, always shooting for the ideal: to be cool, calm, and collected as we confronted and corrected. There were times, however, when confronting and correcting were not enough, and we had to . . .

*Another biblical example of a parent refusing to discipline: "I have warned him that judgment is coming upon his family forever, because his sons are blaspheming God and he hasn't disciplined them" (1 Samuel 3:13 NLT).*

## Enact Consequences When Necessary

Enacting consequences is a biblical idea: "For he who does wrong will receive the consequences of the wrong which he has done, and that without partiality" (Colossians 3:25). This principle easily applies to parenting: wrong behavior habitually shown should receive consequences. Yes, as God extends mercy, grace, and forgiveness, so should we, but that does not absolve a child of consequences for bad behavior any more than God removes consequences for our bad behavior.

For some parents it is tempting to say, "I just don't know what to do." This is just putting one's head in the sand. All kind of help is available. Just Google "age-appropriate consequences" and presto! A stream of excellent and creative information pops up. There are also godly, wise people at church or possibly your child's school who can help you as well as pray for you and your child. Humble yourself and ask for help. Your child's behavior is not unique, and you are not alone.

> *Our heavenly Father allows for consequences: "Well, you've made your bed—now lie in it; you wanted your own way—now, how do you like it?"* (Proverbs 1:31 MSG).

As you search for things that might work for you, keep in mind that suitable consequences fall into two categories: natural and assigned. And also remember, enacting consequences is never done to punish a child. You must be able to say sincerely, "I do this because I love you, not to punish you."

## Natural Consequences: Let Nature Take Its Course

If a child throws his video game on the floor in anger and it breaks, he must learn that he has the power, along with gravity, to destroy his own property. When he does, nature can teach him a lesson. Throw a possession on the floor with great force and it is likely to break. But here is where the parent must come in. When a child destroys his video game in a fit of anger, he loses it. Mom and dad will not buy him another one. Replacing it will come out of *his* money.

Paying for their mistakes out of their own pockets is always a good teacher. A teen who has her second fender bender now contributes money to the natural increased costs of the insurance policy. Her contribution need not be excessive but a sufficient sacrifice to teach her that mistakes can cost dearly. Insurance companies do not say, "No problem," and neither should mom and dad.

I wet the bed until I was eleven. I think the reason it lasted so long is that Mom did not enact natural consequences. When she did, I stopped. My usual routine was to wake up when wetting the bed and then call for my mother. She would change my sheets, help me into dry pajamas, and I would crawl back into bed. Then came the night when I called for Mom and she did not come. I called, "Mom! Mom!" for what seemed to be half an hour, but there was no response.

I got up, went to her bedside, and shook her. "What do you want?" she asked quietly.

"I wet the bed, and you need to help me," I whined.

Mom told me where dry pajamas and sheets were located and that she was not going to help me because, "You can help yourself now."

In literally one night I learned I was fully capable of changing the sheets and my pajamas or suffer the natural consequences of lying there wet the rest of the night. Nature has her ways! That consequence was not inviting. Something clicked in my brain, and I stopped wetting the bed—immediately. (I found out later that a neighbor had told her to try this, and she had hesitated to act on the advice until that fateful night that changed my young life.) Experiencing the natural consequence of wetting my bed was an invaluable gift. Until then I was too embarrassed to stay overnight with friends or sleep outside in a sleeping bag because I knew I would wet myself and be laughed at. Suffering the natural consequences of bed-wetting provided me with a new motivation to change and thus a new freedom. I no longer was enslaved to this behavior. Up to that night Mom had thought she was loving me by helping me. She finally realized she was not helping. She bit the bullet and went through the short-term pain of allowing natural consequences so I could experience the joy of maturing.

In many cases natural consequences can be discipline enough, but as often as not you may have to create or assign a consequence to help your child learn an important lesson.

## Assigned Consequences Should Always Be Logical

Some people call them "logical consequences," but I prefer to call them "assigned consequences," because they are often created to fit the child and situation. I do agree that assigned consequences should be logical in that they must make sense to the parent and the child. (Granted, your child may fail to see your logic, but you must "do as you think best.")

*The Bible says, "Don't hesitate to discipline children. A good spanking won't kill them"* (Proverbs 23:13 GNT).

Based on the severity of the infraction, assigned consequences can be anything from going to their room, doing extra chores, or taking away privileges. For little children some recommend one minute in time-out for each year of the child's age, which is not a bad rule of thumb. To a two-year-old, sitting quietly for two minutes can seem like an eternity and should make your point.

It is important to reinforce the consequence with reasoning as to why it is necessary. Here is a sample note that one father wrote to his ten-year-old: "The way you've been talking to your mother is unacceptable. She is my wife, and I love her. I love you too. In fact, I care so much for you that this hurtful behavior needs to stop because it is hurting everyone. As a consequence, on Saturday, you will cut the grass and rake the leaves, and after that you will help me clean the garage. Love, Dad."

*The apostle Paul acted as a father when he wrote, "I'm not writing all this as a neighborhood scold just to make you feel rotten. I'm writing as a father to you, my children. I love you and want you to grow up well, not spoiled"* (1 Corinthians 4:14 MSG).

When you assign a consequence, you must stick to your guns. A mother wrote, "I try to consider the moment plus the future. If I ground my children for something, I know to stick to it, even with a heavy heart . . . because I know they will get something out of it."

I well recall an instance when Jonathan was a sixteen-year-old, wise in his own eyes. He was being loud and disrespectful and would not stop after I confronted him. So I assigned a simple consequence: "Since you are refusing to stop, here's the deal: every loud, disturbing, disrespectful remark will cost you one dollar out of your savings." He clearly knew better, but something in him rebelled and he made four unacceptable comments, and owed me four dollars. Irked, he pushed the envelope and told me this was stupid, I didn't know how to parent, and any other number of insults. I kept counting out loud, and he didn't think I was for real until we got to twenty-three dollars. At this moment he calmed down enough to realize his stupidity and that he was not in control, nor would he be any day soon. Jonathan knew the rule about respectful speech and suffered the consequences for his foolishness, right where it hurt—in his wallet!

Whether consequences are natural or assigned, do not let them become excessive. For example, when a preschooler absent-mindedly leaves his bike lying in the street and your neighbor runs over it, he is already in enough grief and pain over his loss. He needs your empathy, and some ideas on how he might help earn the price of a new one. And grounding a teenager for a month for missing curfew not only disciplines her excessively but you as well.

Enacting discipline is a parent's toughest job. For this reason we must commit ourselves to this parenting axiom: *I will follow through on these consequences because I love my children too much to let them consciously and willfully disobey what they know is the right thing to do.*

What about the child who respectfully responds to the consequence? Sarah and I tried to focus on the fourth part of our discipline plan.

## Praise and Reward Obedience

Many parents have discipline problems because they focus on correcting the negative behavior but give little thought to bringing a child a "measure of pleasure" for obeying. The child becomes discouraged and thinks, *What's the use? Mom and Dad just think I'm bad anyway.*

As for rewards, charts do wonders for younger children. Many parents use a system that keeps track of how the children obey various rules (cleaning their rooms, making their beds, brushing their teeth), and a certain number of check marks results in a reward of some kind—a sticker, a stick of gum, recognition of some sort that is meaningful to the child. The monetary value is not important; the recognition is the motivator. Think about it: never to reward a child for obeying family rules is like an adult going to work and never receiving a paycheck.[1]

A word of caution: always stress the *why* behind any recognition given. The real motive for obeying should be not to win a prize but because it is the right thing to do. Any reward is just a bonus.

Though we do not reward every positive act, we need to make kids feel good about good behavior if we want them to feel bad about bad behavior. Remember, if all a child perceives is negativity, it only produces more negativity. Try to praise the character quality displayed by the child during or after the time of discipline. Look for ways to say such things as, "I appreciate your self-control" or "your respectfulness" or "your wisdom on how to do it better next time." Then be sure to catch him doing it better next time. "Thanks for doing what I asked without complaining. That is honorable."

## And Reaffirm Love, No Matter What

The final and most important step in our discipline system is reaffirming our love for our kids after discipline is enacted. Sarah and I always tried to work as a team[2] as we would stress the following points:

> "Why do we have rules? Because we love you and want what is best, fair, and safe for you and the whole family."

> "Why do we confront and correct you? Because we love you and do not want you to stray from what is right and necessary."

"Why are there consequences for you at times? Because we love you too much to allow you to ignore our rules and corrections. This would not be best for you or for us."

No family lives by "perfect discipline" that produces "perfect children." Disciplining is doing what "seems best" in each situation, always trying to parent God's way. I have shared our system because it worked for us more often than not. Whenever you discipline your children, try to remember to pray something similar to this:

"Dear Lord, help me to be neither cruel nor permissive, firm but not harsh, fair and consistent, and above all, help me to discipline with love."

---

For more information on the following topics, go to www.loveandrespect.com/parent/discipline:

- Spanking—the why, when, and how
- How to decode before disciplining

# 8

## Encourage

### Equip Them to Succeed
### and Not Lose Heart

To love your children using G-U-I-D-E-S:

How often have you encouraged your children this week? To encourage means, literally: "to give someone courage, to inspire, to embolden, to hearten." Every letter in G-U-I-D-E-S stands for something important to do as a parent, but encouragement can get lost in the shuffle, due to the hustle and bustle of the daily grind and a natural tendency to correct a child's mistakes in an effort to help him improve.

One of the more graphic illustrations of how a parent failed to encourage his child is the story of George Brett, one of the leading major-league hitters of all time, who played for the Kansas City Royals. In 1980, Brett batted .390 and won his second American League batting championship. He went home after the season, and the first thing his dad said was, "You mean to tell me you couldn't have gotten five more hits?" His dad was not content with .390; he wanted his son to bat .400. As usual he was more concerned with what George did not do. "I was always being compared to my three older brothers," George recalled, "and never really got that pat on the back that said, 'You are alright,' and I never, ever did as long as my father was alive."[1]

## The Lord Has Designed All Kids to Need Encouragement

Beware of the trap that may prevent you from giving the encouragement your children desperately need because you are too busy criticizing, being perfectionistic, or pushing them to do better in order to live up to their fullest potential. Many letters I receive from adult children reflect this failure on the part of parents:

> "My father was very critical. He would spend one minute building you up so you could withstand the next fifty-nine minutes while he knocked you down."

> "I excelled in sports, but my dad came to only one basketball game."

> "My father never came to my band concerts, even though I was first chair percussion."

It may look as if fathers are being singled out as the chief culprits in failing to give their kids encouragement, but mothers must also be careful. One young wife wrote to me: "I didn't meet his mom until our wedding. She has always been pleasant to me, but there is not much there with her son: not involved, distant, quiet, no relationship . . . I quickly understood a lot of my husband's cold, stone-like behavior. He explained to me that she always treated him as less than his sister, nothing is good enough, no praise or adoration, negative, sometimes even mean."

There is a hole in the heart of every child that needs filling by loving affirmation from mom and dad. Encouragement is foundational for children to succeed as God intends in this world. The Lord has designed all kids to need encouragement.

Children need to hear us say, "You can do this! You can be that!" They yearn to hear, "Look at what you have done . . . what you have become. Attaboy! Attagirl! God is using you!"

Lack of encouragement can lead to discipline problems. Our children may be reacting to us, not because they are "being bad" but because they feel discouraged and defeated. Do we need to gently inspire or reassure them during challenging moments? Do we need to cheer them on in developing their God-given gifts? Scripture clearly gives us the answer—yes!

*The father of the prodigal looked to inspire his older son: "And he said to him, 'Son, you have always been with me, and all that is mine is yours. But we had to celebrate and rejoice, for this brother of yours was dead and has begun to live, and was lost and has been found'" (Luke 15:31–32).*

## A Parent's Tongue Can Dishearten . . . or Inspire

Even a casual reading of the apostle Paul's writings shows he knew the value of encouragement. When you think about it, every letter he wrote included words to comfort, build up, and inspire. Paul saw himself in the role of a father, reminding the

Thessalonian church how he had been among them, "exhorting and encouraging and imploring each one of you as a father would his own children, so that you would walk in a manner worthy of the God who calls you into His own kingdom and glory" (1 Thessalonians 2:11–12). In 1 Thessalonians 5:14, he gives believers general advice that can easily be applied to children: "Admonish the unruly, encourage the fainthearted, help the weak, be patient with everyone."

Paul knew how fragile children are when he warned parents not to exasperate or embitter their offspring because they can become discouraged or "lose heart" (Colossians 3:21). Parents can say some incredibly mindless, cruel things, as my mail attests.

A daughter remembers her father saying, "You are not worth the gunpowder to blow your brains out."

Another letter shared: "When I was looking for a job, he said, 'Who would hire you?'"

And then there was the daughter who said her alcoholic father told her that: "No man would ever want to touch me or look at me . . . no man would ever love me."

Truly, as James warns, "the tongue is a fire, the very world of iniquity . . . which defiles the entire body, and sets on fire the course of our life, and is set on fire by hell" (James 3:6). Scripture has much to say about restraining one's tongue. Just two examples:

> "The one who guards his mouth preserves his life; the one who opens wide his lips comes to ruin." (Proverbs 13:3)

> "He who guards his mouth and his tongue, guards his soul from troubles." (Proverbs 21:23)

But Scripture also teaches us how to use the tongue in ways that build up, bless . . . and encourage:

> "Pleasant words are a honeycomb, sweet to the soul and healing to the bones." (Proverbs 16:24)

> "Like apples of gold in settings of silver is a word spoken in right circumstances." (Proverbs 25:11)

Author Margie Lewis tells of a father who received a phone call one night from his daughter at college. She had been expelled for breaking the rules. After a long silence he said, "Well, Cindy, I guess you'd better catch the next plane home." He paused, trying to think of a meaningful way to convey the lesson she should learn. Finally, he said, "Remember, when you stand back a distance from a picture, it's usually the dark lines that give it character and beauty."[2]

What a wise, hope-filled statement. This father quietly demonstrated that when a child is not living up to our expectations we can still love, inspire . . . and encourage.

Effective encouragement can be as simple as being more positive with your children. I am not talking about being unrealistic or naive but being able to articulate the problem at hand, communicate a plan to go forward, and instill in them a belief that they can turn the corner. As followers of Jesus Christ,

*David also said to Solomon his son, "Be strong and courageous, and do the work. Do not be afraid or discouraged, for the LORD God, my God, is with you. He will not fail you or forsake you until all the work for the service of the temple of the LORD is finished."*

*—1 Chronicles 28:20 NIV*

we know there is always a way forward. Once again we can take a cue from Paul, who, even when in prison chains, saw his circumstances turning out for the good of the gospel and his Lord Jesus Christ (Philippians 1:12–21). There is always the positive side if we will look for it. I am reminded of the woman who was told she was so optimistic she would see something good in the devil himself. She replied instantly, "Well, he *is* persistent!"[3]

As I look back on how Sarah and I tried to encourage our children, I can think of three major areas where we concentrated our efforts:

- Encourage them as life happens.
- Encourage who they are and what they do.
- Encourage who and what they can become.

Following are some observations, stories, and suggestions on each of these three key areas.

## Encourage Them as Life Happens and They Face Challenges and Fears

Encouraging your child simply means coming near to your son or daughter, especially when he or she is losing heart, and giving that child hope, comfort, and reassurance in a world that does not always make sense. Most parents do this quite naturally when their children are infants and very young, but as more children arrive, the older ones may struggle because they feel lost in the shuffle. This was true of our middle child, David, when he was around seven. His older brother, Jonathan, was ignoring him and his younger sister, Joy, was getting most of the attention as the baby of the family. I could tell he was feeling left out. One day, while we were wandering through some gift shops during a vacation at Disney World, I came upon a glass teddy bear piggy bank with the name "David" on his chest.

"David, look at this teddy bear bank," I said. "I am buying this for you. You are Daddy's special teddy bear. No one else is my special teddy bear but you."

David just beamed, and all that day and for many days afterward, he kept asking, "Am I your special teddy bear and no one else?" I still have that teddy bear piggy bank sitting on a shelf in my office. I am sure it meant a lot to David when he was young and in need of encouragement, but now I am sure it means more to me. The point is, look for needs in your children. Be aware of their interests, their concerns, and especially the challenges or problems that life is throwing at them. There are dozens of ways to encourage them—a simple word or pat on the back, a special little gift, such as a teddy bear, or perhaps taking them on a special excursion. It does not have to be elaborate or expensive. What they need is you—your interest, your concern, your *time*—anything that tells them that Mom or Dad says, "I love you. I am for you. You are important to me."

Sometimes you can give them encouragement even when they do not seem to want it. My mother was good at that with me. One major example is when I enrolled in military school in the eighth grade. Initially, I was all for it as I flipped through the catalog countless times admiring the different uniforms, marching formations, and the rifles and swords. When I arrived I expected to have a great adventure, but within a few weeks I was overwhelmed with homesickness and pleaded with Mom on the phone to let me quit and come home. It took her totally by surprise. My dad, as usual, never got involved. But instead of giving up and giving in to my tearful requests, she told me she knew this was hard for me, but that I should hang in there, and she would think about what could be done.

She then called the commandant of the military school, Colonel Bailey, and asked for his counsel. That call led to Colonel Bailey meeting personally with me. He did not dress me down; instead, he empathetically encouraged me, letting me know that what I was feeling was quite normal and would soon pass. He told me not to quit but to take it a day at a time and see what happened. He talked to me man-to-man and told me "these are things we must go through in becoming a man."

Colonel Bailey's advice was not easy for a very homesick thirteen-year-old to hear. At the same time, knowing my mom and the colonel both empathized with me and that what I was feeling was nothing out of the ordinary relieved me a great deal. I stuck it out, got past the homesickness, and stayed in school. To this day I am extremely grateful that Mom did not let her nurturing nature melt her heart to give in to my tearful pleas. She had the courage to go to someone with the knowledge to help—Colonel Bailey—and with his encouragement she was able to encourage me at a crucial time in my life to help me get past my fears. I needed to learn not to quit when overwhelmed by something I could not control. I stayed in military school for five years and graduated with many honors—an experience God used to set the course of my life.

I share this story to encourage parents in the very delicate area of when to allow their child to quit. Perhaps you could use the counsel of a knowledgeable, empathetic person to help you and your child with a crisis of one kind or another right now. It can be embarrassing to ask for advice, but momentary pride should give way to what is best for your child. If that means turning to your neighbor, friend, fellow church member, youth pastor, or whomever, so be it. As the Preacher said, "There is nothing new under the sun" (Ecclesiastes 1:9). Everything we may experience as we parent our kids has happened to other parents, somewhere, sometime. We owe it to ourselves and our children to explore these resources.

# When Should You Allow Your Child to Quit?

If quitting something becomes a serious option, when should it be allowed? Sarah and I followed no hard-and-fast rules when it came to parenting our kids; it depended on what it was—quitting a sports team, dropping a class, leaving camp early, ending the paper route—we dealt with all of these and more. We did have one general goal: our children should finish what they start, and if they do quit, it should be at natural transition points, such as the end of the season or school year. Quitting should not happen on impulse, and whining or wailing are not allowed to manipulate us into a hasty decision.

> *The Bible provides us with principles to guide our parenting: "A person's anxiety will weigh him down, but an encouraging word makes him joyful"* (Proverbs 12:25 GW).

Keep in mind, children are different, and their individual needs and capabilities must enter in. However, fulfilling one's commitments is an important lesson for all children to learn.

Jonathan had a paper route he started during his sophomore year in high school. He kept it going faithfully until his junior year, when a lot of school activities began to take his time. He felt he should give up the paper route, even though it provided good spending money. We determined that he was not being irresponsible but actually wanting to be more responsible in other, more important areas. Kids can get overextended (as can adults), and some things should go for the good of all concerned.

Having said this, children do not always want to be responsible and will take the easy way out if they can. The parent's job is to help them see the value in finishing what they start and to use the opportunity to encourage a child to grow—perhaps a little, perhaps a lot (as was the case with me in military school).

As your children grow up and face different challenges, always try to explain, at their level of understanding, why you encourage them in doing hard or tough things. You can say something similar to, "There are always things that are hard, things that we don't want to do. We know what it is like because adults have to face lots of hard things too. We're encouraging you to stay with it in these tough times so you can grow in wisdom and strength and be better prepared for the future."

It is especially important to encourage and build up our kids when they fail. That is when we need to move in and act as cheerleaders. Parents are the ones who can see the good in their children, even if the whole world seems to have walked out on them. We are the ones who must tell them: "You are dependable . . . you are honest . . . we believe in you . . . God is for you, and so are we!"

## Encourage Who They Are and What They Do

Always be looking for how God has wired each of your children with a unique temperament, along with certain spiritual gifts and interests. Verify and reinforce what you see with your comments, for example: "Mom and I appreciate watching how you enjoy people and that you love having people around." "We see you have the gift of mercy and believe God gave you that gift. You really care about the feelings of others." "You have a real aptitude and interest in mechanical things. That is fantastic!"

Also look for instances when you "catch them doing something right" and tell them so. Do not just take their good choices for granted; affirm them with compliments and positive observations. "Kelly, thank you so much for sitting and talking with Grandma while I ran that errand. You blessed her heart . . . and mine too." A dad realizes his son has an ability to avoid and solve conflicts while playing with his friends. He tells him: "I noticed yesterday when you made a deal with Ben to play a board game for a while and then switch to building a fort, which is much more your thing. I like the way you handle things like that." A mom observes her daughter resolving a problem with her friend and avoiding hurt feelings and comments: "Honey, I watched the way you were a peacemaker with Chelsea. She was pretty upset, but you came up with a way to be friends again. I am really impressed!"

There are times, of course, when you must discipline or correct them if they are being disrespectful or inconsiderate, but even then it is possible to be encouraging. If a nine-year-old boy calls his little sister names, dad can step in and say: "Jeremy, I know you want to grow to be a man of honor. Men of honor don't call people names."

These examples acknowledge a child's character as well as gifts and aptitudes. Encouraging character traits such as diligence, honesty, helpfulness, fairness, serving others, perseverance, and being teachable and respectful will actually help our children develop these qualities. Remember, what we believe children to be, they often become.

When our Jonathan was a preschooler, he came out of his

Sunday school class looking sheepish. He had taken from the class a toy car he had been playing with. I could tell he knew this was wrong, so I explained, "This toy does not belong to you. We don't take things that do not belong to us. We must always be honest. We are men of integrity. Let's take the toy back." Jonathan did not know the full meaning of words such as *integrity*, but I kept reinforcing them whenever I could, praising him during moments he showed integrity and honesty. A few years later Jonathan and his younger brother, David, got in an argument about what had happened at a certain event. David was so sure he was right he called Jonathan a liar, who coolly replied, "I am not. I am a man of integrity and always will be."

Keep Proverbs 20:11 in mind: "It is by his deeds that a lad distinguishes himself if his conduct is pure and right." This certainly applies to girls as well. Kids do show who they are by what they do, how they act. Let them know when they have distinguished themselves with good conduct. It is all too easy to comment only on what needs correcting: "Sit up straight . . . don't stuff your mouth . . . say 'thank you'"—the list is endless. Develop another list of positive affirmations: "What you did was outstanding . . . I appreciate your helpfulness . . . Thanks for responding with such respect . . . I love your attitude . . . great job." Work on phrases that fit each of your children, according to age, gender, and where they need encouraging the most. (See chapter 11 on the difference between parenting girls and boys.)

Mark it down: encouragement given authentically and sincerely is hard to resist and definitely influences your children, even if they don't seem to notice. Believe me; they *are* noticing and remembering what you say.

# Encourage Who and What They Can Become

What do you hope your children will become when they grow up? Ask that question of parents, and you will get all kinds of answers. The mother of two daredevil boys might just smile and say, "Well . . . at the moment I am concentrating on hoping they live long enough to grow up." Other parents would answer with detailed descriptions of what they think their kids should do and be.

In his excellent book *How to Really Love Your Child*, Dr. Ross Campbell identifies a common type of inappropriate parental love for a child as vicariousness: trying to live your life or dreams through the life of your child. For example, "A mother does this by steering her daughter [or son] into . . . situations where she herself longs to be."[4] This is not encouragement but a parent's manipulation for self-serving purposes.

I heard of a mother who threw a fit when her daughter's kindergarten teacher chose another child for the lead part in a little play the class was going to present.

> *Then the mother of the sons of Zebedee came to Jesus with her sons, bowing down and making a request of Him. And He said to her, "What do you wish?" She said to Him, "Command that in Your kingdom these two sons of mine may sit one on Your right and one on Your left."*
>
> —Matthew 20:20–21

It was painfully obvious that the real issue was not her child, but her own ego. Unfortunately, her self-centered reaction taught her daughter the wrong lesson: when you *lose* at something, you need to be offended and incensed, rather than learn the better lesson of losing graciously and being supportive of others.

We assure ourselves we would never act like that, but the question is still worth asking: What is our real motive for encouraging our children in certain endeavors? Some parents are so concerned for their child's feelings of being accepted and popular that they become obsessed with orchestrating their successes. Do we want our kids to have courage to deal confidently with life as God intends, or are we really manipulating them to perform well for the world so they can feel good about themselves . . . or, even worse, so we can feel good about ourselves? Not a few children act up because they perceive their parents' encouragement as manipulation, not motivation.

Some parents try to motivate their children to succeed in areas beyond their inherited skills or aptitudes. Too often, parents want their kids to succeed where they have failed, which in some strange way may make the parents feel better about themselves.

I know of one woman who was told by her father she "would not amount to very much" because she did not excel in subjects he thought important, including math. The woman eventually married and became a successful professional in the caring industry, known for her extraordinary compassion for people in need. Did this incredibly gifted professional learn from her experience when she became a wife and mother? No, in fact the cycle continues. Now she has a son who lacks skill in math but has great social skills. Much as her father did, she gripes about her son's math scores while ignoring his obvious gifts in interacting with people and responding to human needs.

Then we have the other scenario, where a parent who does excel in a certain area, such as music, academics, or sports, expects his child to have the same gifts. We need to be sensitive to our children as uniquely gifted beings, not our clones, who need to be encouraged in the areas that bring them joy. To do otherwise will eventually backfire—sometimes much later in life. I counseled a dentist who told me, "I am a nineteen-year-old in a forty-year-old man's body. I decided at nineteen to be a dentist because my dad was a dentist. At forty, I am a dentist because a nineteen-year-old kid and his dad decided this for me. I am miserable."

Scripture is very clear. We all have certain gifts (Romans 12:6–8; 1 Corinthians 12). As parents we should encourage the gifts we see in our children, just as Paul encouraged Timothy not to neglect the spiritual gift within him (1 Timothy 4:14; 2 Timothy 1:6). Yes, math and English are very important, but even more important is how God has gifted each one of us. Early in each child's life we must detect God's design and steer him accordingly.

Be encouraged by what Scripture says and keep letting your child know you are confident "that he who began a good work in [him] will carry it on to completion" (Philippians 1:6 NIV). Have faith that God has called your children and has instilled desires in them to serve His kingdom. Let your kids know you are praying for them, "asking our God to enable [them] to live a life worthy of his call. May he give you the power to accomplish all the good things your faith prompts you to do" (2 Thessalonians 1:11 NLT). Trust that God has planted a seed in your child's heart and that you can water it. Believe there is a desire God intends to fulfill and reinforce this at every opportunity.

When Joy was ten, she exhibited some entrepreneurial skills in starting her own little neighborhood business. We supported her with encouragement and helped her distribute a leaflet throughout our neighborhood. The leaflet, which she wrote herself, gave her age and contact information and also stated: "I am available to do things that may help you out . . . walk your dog or cat, feed your pets, water your plants, help bring in groceries, sweep your porch or front steps . . . watch your preschoolers while you get some things done . . . I like to help out!" Joy got several jobs through her little ad, and today she shows the same kind of helping-out initiative as she works for Love and Respect Ministries to reach her generation with the Love & Respect message. And, oh yes, she thoroughly loves what she is doing, though she no longer walks dogs—but does kill plants! In fact, she told me recently, "I still reminisce about how the dog walking and plant watering was far more lucrative than my current gig with you."

I urge you to increase and perfect your efforts at praising and encouraging your children, but always seek a balance. It is possible to praise too much, especially if we are focusing on their performance. Jonathan recalls wanting a few more doses of reality and constructive criticism. ("I knew I wasn't really *that* good.") David pointed out praise has limited effect when the child knows that is all he will hear. ("If you say, 'Great job!' whenever I do *anything*, it means nothing.")

Make a decision to be an encouraging parent because you believe that God has given your children talents and spiritual gifts for His purposes. As the Lord intends to use us, He intends to use our children. What a joy to encourage our believing children to kindle the gifts that God imparted to them (2 Timothy 1:6) and not to bury their talents (Matthew 25:15–28).

A plaque I had on my wall while the children grew up has the following maxim etched in the wood:

> *Seeing good where there was no*
> *good except in* **His** *seeing.*

This comes from a larger idea that people who encourage others see the good and giftedness in us before we see these things in ourselves. Yet their belief in us gives us the courage and

confidence to develop what they see in us. That is encouragement—
and that is real parental love.

———

For more information on the following topics, go to
www.loveandrespect.com/parent/encouragement:

- Encouraging our kids as God encourages us
- Encouraging our kids in the face of life's unanswered
  questions
- Looking for my child's natural bent
- Just showing up can make all the difference
- What is flattery and its downside?

# 9

## SUPPLICATE

## Pray . . . with Confidence That God Listens to Us and Speaks to Them

To love your children using G-U-I-D-E-S:
Though Supplication is the last letter in G-U-I-D-E-S, it is far from being the least important principle in parenting God's way. To supplicate means "to ask or petition for humbly and earnestly." As parents we have the privilege of praying routinely for our children, especially as it relates to G-U-I-D-E-S:

- When you Give, pray that God helps your child have a *thankful and grateful heart.*
- When you Understand, pray that God helps your child have a *calm and tranquil heart.*
- When you Instruct, pray that God helps your child have a *teachable spirit.*
- When you Discipline, pray that God helps your child *have true remorse.*

- When you **E**ncourage, pray that God helps your child *to have courage.*
- When you **S**upplicate, pray that God helps your child have a *trusting and obedient heart.*

Parents who believe in Jesus recognize their limitations. They need Jesus to do what they cannot: bless, heal, change, and strengthen their children. For believing parents there is great comfort when relying on the Lord in prayer and supplication. In the Gospels we see parents bring their children "to Jesus for him to place his hands on them and pray for them" (Matthew 19:13 NIV; see also Mark 10:13; Luke 18:15). In other instances parents asked Jesus to heal or restore their children. For example, the royal official asked healing for his mortally ill son (John 4:46–49); the synagogue official asked Jesus to restore his dead daughter (Matthew 9:18–26); and the father asked for mercy for his demon-possessed son (Matthew 17:14–18).

In all these biblical scenes parents earnestly and humbly petitioned the Lord to touch and heal their kids. This is supplication in its most heartwarming, instructive, and compelling form. Just as the Lord welcomed these parents and prayed for their children, He welcomes you and your children with the same blessings and help. Make Psalm 86:6 your own petition: "Give ear, O LORD, to my prayer; and give heed to the voice of my supplications!"[1]

## Praying for Yourself First

Each letter in the G-U-I-D-E-S acronym also suggests a prayer request for ourselves as we ask God's help to parent His way. We can pray, "Lord, may we . . .

- **G**ive with a spirit of generosity.
- **U**nderstand with empathy.
- **I**nstruct with wisdom.
- **D**iscipline with fairness.
- **E**ncourage with discernment.
- **S**upplicate with faith.

We can also pray for wisdom to decode our kids and ourselves when they feel unloved and we feel disrespected, and then pray for help as we defuse the potential craziness. Let's keep the ideas of decoding and defusing on our prayer list with the confidence that the Lord loves us and hears our supplications. I suggest writing down the titles of section heads in this book that inspired you and pray based on these, such as, "Lord, help me reassure my child of my love."

Granted, all this is a tall order. Will you fail? Of course, and then you fall back on Proverbs 24:16: "For a righteous man falls seven times, and rises again." Also take comfort in knowing that the Helper—the Holy Spirit—is there to guide and empower you. Sarah and I look humbly every day to God's Spirit to help us. Without Him, we could not have parented our kids God's way as they grew up, and we still need His wisdom as they have moved into adult lives of their own.

Please believe me: your children want you to pray for them, and not doing so can have a profound negative effect, as one man in his sixties testified when he told

*No matter the outcome, believing parents have always prayed for their children. "David prayed to God that the child would get well. He refused to eat anything, and every night he went into his room and spent the night lying on the floor"* (2 Samuel 12:16 GNT).

me, "I never heard my dad pray once." As I talked with him, I learned he had felt unimportant and unloved all his life. His dad's prayers could have made a big difference, as illustrated in a letter I received from another man in my church:

> I remember in high school getting up early to go running at 6 a.m. There in the living room I found my dad kneeling at the couch. Later that day I asked him about it, and he told me that he woke up every weekday at 5:30 a.m. to pray and read the Word for an hour. I had no idea that he prayed for us. I've been so fortunate to have a dad who recognizes his absolute dependency on the Lord. My dad's example is a constant reminder and challenge to me.

I believe this dad prayed about things related to G-U-I-D-E-S, though he did not know of our acronym. Such parents know the Scriptures related to parenting and turn these passages into petitions. For example, parents will find themselves praying, "Lord, because of what You tell me in Ephesians 6:4 and Colossians 3:21, help me not to provoke or exasperate my children." These parents know that when they pray based on the Bible, God hears them (1 John 5:14–15).

## Using Scripture to Pray for Our Kids

There is no prayer formula for parents and no absolute guarantee God will answer just as we might wish. However, the will of God can be found in the Word of God. When we come across a passage that talks about children, we can turn His Word into a prayer, trusting God to hear us supplicating according to His will. Following are some specific ways to pray for your children based on Scripture passages.

*Pray that they will experience saving faith in Christ.* Salvation was primary for the apostle Paul. He envisioned a child's upbringing in the Scriptures leading to the eternal salvation that came though faith in Jesus Christ (2 Timothy 3:15). Paul knew the absolute importance of praying for another's salvation (Romans 10:1), and we must pray this way for our children, that they would encounter the living Christ and believe in Him. God desires all people—especially our children—to be saved (1 Timothy 2:4; 2 Peter 3:9). This should be our primary petition for our children while putting them in situations to hear this good news.

The Lord orchestrated this with our daughter, Joy. She shared how she believed at the tender age of five:

> Many people think that young children who come to know the Lord don't actually have a true conversion experience and that they only believe because of the way they were raised. For some this may be true. I was a pastor's child and had obviously heard about Jesus. But as a five-year-old, watching *The Jesus Film* in the church office while my dad worked in his study nearby, I specifically remember something clicking in my brain and heart. Luke 10:21 talks about how truths can be revealed to infants, which means the redemption story of Christ is actually quite simple—and I got it, as a five-year-old. I knew that before me was a Man who loved me so much that He would die for me. I also had the understanding that I wasn't perfect, and yet He still did that for me out of love. It just made sense. And I believed.

*Pray that they will learn and love the Bible.* When Paul wrote in 2 Timothy 3:15, "from childhood you have known the Holy Scriptures, which are able to make you wise for salvation" (NKJV), he brought to light the essential role of the Bible. Reading Bible stories to your little ones in a spirit of prayer, asking God to touch and open their hearts, is a beautiful way to "make [them] wise for salvation" at an early age. As they grow, continue to pray that God's Spirit will enlighten their hearts to His truth as they read the Bible and hear it being taught (Ephesians 1:18).

Continually work on being an example of someone who reads, studies, and appreciates Scripture. My graduate school research among adult children from Christian homes included this question: "What are some specific activities your father did to contribute to your Christian growth?" Their responses were peppered with phrases like these: "daily Bible reading . . . family devotions . . . did devotions with me . . . memorizing verses with me . . . modeled a daily quiet time . . . devotions with prayer every night . . ."[2]

> *And give to my son Solomon a perfect heart to keep Your commandments.*
>
> —1 Chronicles 29:19

Suppose, however, you have not been that much of a model of Bible reading and devotions. Do not let guilt weigh you down. I have my own story in this regard. I did not fail to read Scripture, since I studied it thirty hours a week for twenty years as a pastor. Where I failed was not sharing more with my kids of my own deep feelings from what I learned in my pastor's study. I assumed that if they saw me from the pulpit, conveying my heart and emotions in my preaching, it would spill over onto them. The Spirit of God refreshed my soul in my study countless times, and I wept for joy, but my children rarely saw this. In trying to avoid overwhelming them with Scripture, I often neglected to share with them personally what Scripture had said to me or how God used me in my office as I led people to Christ.

I share this personal glimpse to encourage you to express to your children from your heart what God has been saying to you through His Word. Kids often become fans of the same sports teams their mom and dad cheer for enthusiastically. The same can hold true as they hear their parents expressing real love and enthusiasm for God's Word, the pastor's message, or answers to prayer. Your kids can sense what you truly value by what really excites you, and are far more likely to want to emulate what mom and dad see as "the real deal." Pray that your heart comes through to your kids and that their hearts respond (Malachi 4:6).

*Pray that your kids will experience the love of the indwelling Christ.* Many adults testify: "I asked Jesus into my heart, but nothing much happened after that." God intends so much more! Jesus prayed to the Father for the disciples, asking "that the love with which You loved Me may be in them, and I in them" (John 17:26; see also Ephesians 3:17, 19).

Sarah and I would try to turn our reading of Scripture into prayers for our kids when the text struck us as pertinent. For instance, we might pray that the kids would abide in Jesus based on what the apostle John wrote: "Now, little children, abide in Him, so that when He appears, we may have confidence and not shrink away from Him in shame at His coming" (1 John 2:28). Or we might pray that the kids would allow the power of Christ in them to help them overcome the dark forces of the world. "You are from God, little children, and have overcome them; because greater is He who is in you than he who is in the world" (1 John 4:4).

Authentic faith within our children makes all the difference in the world. A parent wrote me that although the teasing her autistic son endured in kindergarten is still with him, now at age ten he deals with it much better. She added: "We always tried to turn his thoughts to loving them with the love of Jesus and to help him understand that these children didn't have the love of Jesus in their hearts and needed Him. His whole life changed when he accepted the Lord in first grade, and he has taken this view ever since."[3]

What strength and peace can come to our children when Christ takes up residence within them (Colossians 1:27). We must petition our Lord to help our children make Him number one in their lives and enjoy all the benefits of knowing Him. Look for opportunities to help your children apply their faith to their everyday circumstances.

*Pray that you do not hinder their faith.* All parents need to pray fervently that they do not undermine a child's dependency on Christ. Jesus had strong words against this: "Whoever causes one of these little ones who believe in Me to stumble, it would be better for him to have a heavy millstone hung around his neck, and to be drowned in the depth of the sea" (Matthew 18:6). A major motivation for Sarah and me to help couples with their marriages is knowing how harmful it is when mom and dad are always on the Crazy Cycle. (See chapter 14 for more on how serious it is to "cause a little one to stumble.")

> A mother wrote: My daughter called and was complaining about her life. I suggested that she needed to look to God for answers. She let me know that she has lost a lot of her faith because of how she has viewed our marriage relationship . . . it grieves me to see how it affects our daughters and their relationships because of what they have lived and learned.

Contrast this with the testimony of a dad: "I have noticed that in trying to show love to my wife, avoiding yelling and anger and being more encouraging (none of this perfectly, though), my kids have responded. I have had more conversations about God and the Bible with my twelve-year-old son, which is an incredible blessing."

## Your Kids Are Watching

There are several things we can do to make sure our kids not only are prayed for but also are learning about an effective prayer life.

*Do not hide how you go to God in prayer.* Though we are to pray in our closets (Matthew 6:6), the kids need to know we are in the closet. I heard the story of a dad who was a policeman. His routine each evening when he arrived home was to go change his clothes and then spend time alone in prayer with God. The kids knew that daddy was talking to God, and afterward he would play with them. What a beautiful approach to prayer. While needing God for his transition back into family life from a day exposed to crime, he also demonstrated that a strong man still depends on almighty God.

Sarah models prayer and thanksgiving. In 2004, an oncologist diagnosed her with breast cancer. After praying and getting the best medical advice, Sarah decided that a double mastectomy and reconstruction would best remedy her cancerous condition. Years later her judgment proved correct. However, at the time she did not know if she would live or die, especially since four years earlier her mother had died of cancer three weeks after the diagnosis.

Hundreds watched Sarah. She did not shake her fist at God and ask, "Why me?" Instead she asked, "Why *not* me?"

Then in the midst of her cancer, Sarah did the remarkable. Like King David, she thanked and praised God, an all-loving and all-powerful God. As a family we observed Sarah as she looked forward to her morning time alone with God, enjoyed listening to her praise music, told others of God's goodness, and evidenced throughout the day an inner peace.

> We prayed that he would give us and our children a safe journey. We asked him to keep safe everything we owned.
>
> —Ezra 8:21 NIRV

Sarah's example caused all of us to examine our hearts: Would we trust, thank, praise, and worship God at the possibility of death's door?

A friend told me how his dad's earlier life and sunset years have affected him to this day:

Every noon, he read a chapter of Scripture. He'd say to me, "Get the book." No matter who was there, he'd read a chapter. He'd also ask a question at the end. When he was older, living with me as an aged man, I'd walk into his room, and there he was on his knees praying. He wasn't verbal. We did not discuss issues deeply. But Dad had a deep faith that was very much part of his life.

*Pray with and for your children.* My research on families included asking children what they remembered about how their parents prayed for them. Comments included: "He prayed with me and for me and set an example." "We all prayed together daily." "We prayed before meals and they prayed with us at night." "He is always praying for me and talking about God's direction for my life."

With our own kids, Sarah and I tried to personalize our

prayers for each of them, according to their abilities, interests, and personalities. For example, when Jonathan was younger, we may have prayed something such as this:

> Lord, I thank You for Jonathan. I thank You for the ability You have given to him to play sports and the joy this brings to him and his teammates. I thank You for his diligence in studying for school and what he is learning, particularly his interest in history. Thank You for his paper route and his consistency in getting up early to deliver papers. Thank You for the way he serves his customers.

That kind of prayer fit Jonathan, and he appreciated it. Try developing personalized prayers for each of your children, which will be much more meaningful than the old generic: "Bless the kids today, Lord. Amen."

When our kids were younger, we used the bedtime routine as a perfect opportunity for prayers. They welcomed this because it was a way to make "staying up" last a few minutes longer.

Steven Curtis Chapman, with whom I shared the stage at an outdoor festival in Kansas, related this story about his kids to the crowd: He and his wife were hurrying to leave for the evening, and he was trying to get them to say their prayers and get to bed. With mom and dad all dressed up to go out, excitement filled the air, and the kids did their best to stall by praying "around the world" for everything they could think of. Finally, Steven said firmly, "We're only praying for the family tonight!"

*Do not pray at them.* Always guard against using prayer as a way of sending a message to a child to perform. Remember that you are talking to the Lord, not your kids. This can be a subtle yet manipulative ploy that will sour your kids toward prayer.

*Share with your children what God teaches you through your prayers.* Following is a story we would often tell our kids over the years. With this story we instructed them that trusting God does work, and they could trust Him with their needs too.

In 1975, when I was fresh out of seminary, I joined another pastor in launching a Christian counseling center called The Open Door. We did not charge for our counseling, nor did we solicit donations for support. Instead we emulated the eighteenth-century English missionary George Mueller, whose orphanage ministry raised 1.4 million pounds (over $7 million in today's dollars), even though Mueller never made his needs known to anyone but God alone.[4]

The first year we set a modest budget, and every month the finances rolled in like clockwork. We were thrilled and a bit awed, but in faith we raised our budget for the second year. Support kept coming—until April, when we came up seven hundred dollars short with bills that had to be paid. I confess. I was very angry because now critics of our faith venture could crow about how we had failed.

My partner, older in years and the faith, suggested that we pray, and we did so, acknowledging before God that He had promised to meet our needs and thanking Him for hearing our request for seven hundred dollars. I also confessed my immaturity, anxiety, and ungratefulness. We concluded our prayer by thanking Him for His faithfulness and expressing our confidence in Him to support The Open Door as He deemed appropriate.

Then we went home.

The next day back at the office, my partner said, "Do you remember that schoolteacher who recently divorced with four children, and I led her to Christ?"

I replied, "Yes."

"Well," he explained, "last night she knocked on our door and handed me a check for six hundred dollars!"

We both rejoiced in prayer over this totally unexpected gift. With our faith bolstered we "reminded" God that we needed a hundred dollars more. A bit later I went to the mailbox and found an unmarked, unsealed envelope. It contained four twenties and one ten. We were just ten dollars short of the seven hundred.

That same day an elderly retired schoolteacher came by and asked, "Do you boys take donations?" (She had read about The Open Door ministry in the paper, but nothing had been mentioned about donations.) We assured her we did, and she handed us a check for ten dollars, explaining that she was on a monthly fixed income but still always tried to give five dollars above her tithes to worthy organizations. As she had driven to our office, the Lord had spoken to her heart saying, "Double it!"

*Parents give their children full reports on your faithful ways.*

—Isaiah 38:19 MSG

We thanked her profusely, and I was grinning from ear to ear, although I felt a bit sheepish for my anger and unbelief the previous night. Indeed, the Lord had taught me an unforgettable lesson about praying and trusting Him. It is a lesson I have passed on to my children, always explaining that God is powerful, and when we pray, it can unleash that power. While it happened long ago, it affects our family even today, reminding all of us of the power of prayer.

What has God taught you about trusting Him? As you encounter God through prayer, don't contain your excitement; let it spill over onto the rest of your family, as one mom did:

I started praying for the first time in years and began attending church also. Today, I do not like to miss any of the services and strive to read my Bible and release myself to His guidance. One of my most requested prayers was to better understand what has happened in my life . . . God led me to *Love & Respect*, which provided me with the answer to my prayer for understanding. The end of the book talked about eternal life and was so inspiring I made a commitment right then and there to live my life fully for God.

I decided to be baptized. I called all my family to ask them to attend, to witness my new start in life. Another answer to my prayers is all three of my boys are going with me. When I called my oldest son, twenty-four, he shared with me his desire to also be baptized. My joy and happiness swelled my heart more than I have words to explain. He is returning to Iraq in approximately a month for a second tour of duty. This helped ease the worry in my heart. God is also working in my other sons' lives.

When a parent has authentic faith and is enjoying the Lord, it's contagious!

## Your Prayer Life Reveals What You Really Believe

To help your prayer life be contagious, meditate on Scriptures that talk to you about how to pray. Commit a passage, James 1:5–6, for example, to memory: "But if any of you lack wisdom, you should pray to God, who will give it to you; because God gives generously and graciously to all. But when you pray, you must believe and not doubt at all" (GNT). James is urging us to truly believe that God will give us wisdom to deal with all the trials we face, and that surely includes those in the family. Raising children is an endless and often stressful task; there are many blessings, yes, but there are many troubles and trials. The troubles may at times seem to outweigh the blessings.

*All through the night get up again and again to cry out to the Lord; Pour out your heart and beg him for mercy on your children.*

*—Lamentations 2:19 GNT*

This passage is not promising that everything will go perfectly but that we will be given wisdom to deal with every situation. God gives us wisdom, but note the major condition: that we do not doubt. Doubt can send us into uncertainty, worry, anxiety—what James calls double-mindedness that leaves us unstable and unsure (James 1:6–8). Remember Hebrews 12:9–10? As we follow Christ we must in good faith "do what seems best" and trust God for His wisdom.

It is in the problem moments of parenting that your prayer life will reveal what you really believe about the character of God. Do you really want His wisdom? When you faithfully pray for wisdom in all trying circumstances, you are declaring that you believe God is for you and loves you and your kids, no matter what happens.

Whatever your situation—married with a spouse who prays with you, married but having to deal with a lot of the parenting yourself, or fighting the single-parent battle—never let prayer slip. We are to pray because Jesus prayed. He is our example, and our teacher of how to pray—not in showy pretense but in your "closet": a quiet place where you can share your needs, as well as your praises and thankfulness (Matthew 6:5–6).

Yes, there are always busy, hectic, chaotic times, when going to your quiet place just is not possible, but never neglect prayer because you are *too busy*. Pray on the run, as you deal with the next dirty diaper, the next glass of spilled milk, the next broken window, or the next missed curfew. Make Luke 18:1–8 a passage to remember. Jesus told His disciples the parable of the persistent widow "to show them that they should always pray and not give up" (v. 1 NIV).

My grandmother is an example of a woman who never gave up on prayer. As she raised her family on the farmlands of South Dakota in the early 1900s, my grandmother always sought God's wisdom, even when He did not seem to hear. Her husband died during the infamous flu epidemic of 1918, when their tiny son, my father, was only three months old. My father grew up watching his mother live out her faith, praying in every circumstance for their needs and believing that in all things her heavenly Father was working for the good of her family (Romans 8:28). During the Depression of the 1930s, she sold her home and gave the money to Faith Home, a Christian orphanage and Bible school. Despite his mother's example and prayers, my father left home at eighteen, leaving his faith as well.

For years my father stayed away from the church. Even after marriage and children, he never talked to us about Jesus Christ. Never! It sounds as if my grandmother's prayers were for naught, but not so. I came to Christ at age sixteen, and two years later so did my mother, my sister, and my dad!

After he came to Christ at age fifty-one, my father expressed sorrow for walking away from his mother's faith and wasting so many years, but he rejoiced in God's kindness to all of our family because of his mother's supplications. After I entered the ministry, knowing a little about his story, I asked him, "Do you think the Spirit of God skipped over you because you resisted the Lord and landed on me because of your mother's prayers?"

His quick reply: "Absolutely!" Then in one of the most significant exchanges we ever had, he added: "I do believe that the Lord came to you because of your grandmother's prayers for me—which I resisted. I don't understand these things, but I have felt in my heart that the Lord touched you because of my mother's prayers and the prayers of others who prayed with her."

I never knew my grandmother. She transitioned to heaven before I was born. Were her prayers for her son answered? To echo my dad, "Absolutely!" Her story is a striking example of parenting God's way, praying for your children in obedience to Christ's command, and trusting your heavenly Father for wisdom, whatever the outcome.

---

For more information on the following topics, go to www.loveandrespect.com/parent/supplication:

- Three vital questions concerning prayer
- Can we pray too much for our kids?
- Younger kids' love for prayer at bedtime
- How our postmodern culture undermines trust in prayer
- How to pray to stand against the devil's wiles

# 10

## TEAMWORK

### *How to Put Your Children First*

Okay, time for a quick parental quiz: What impacts your children more? Your relationship with your spouse or your relationship with your children?

Because we have just spent the last six chapters discussing different skills to improve our parenting, it would be easy enough to say, "My relationship with my children." But after counseling married couples for more than thirty-five years, it is my conviction that your relationship with your spouse—the strength of your marriage—equally impacts your children. The marriage is the backside of the parenting coin.

The last prophet in the Old Testament was Malachi, who brought God's word to the Jews around 430 BC. They had returned from captivity; the temple had been rebuilt as well as Jerusalem's walls. The Jews had indeed been blessed, but in typical fashion they had already started to fall away from true worship and were living in disobedience to the Lord. Neglect of marriage, intermarriage with unbelievers, and divorce were all rampant. As Malachi thundered God's displeasure with all the broken marriages, he wrote: "Has not the LORD made them one? In flesh and spirit they are his. And why one? Because he was seeking godly offspring" (Malachi 2:15 NIV).

Godly offspring were so important to the Lord He did not want parents to split up (Malachi 2:16). He knows—far beyond what we can imagine—what harm divorce can do to families and His kingdom. Jesus echoed this same truth during His own ministry. When the Pharisees tried to get Him into a corner by asking Him when it was lawful for a man to divorce his wife, Jesus went back to the beginning to underscore the sacred importance of marriage: God made them male and female and when a man left father and mother to be united to his wife they became "one flesh . . . they are no longer two, but one" (Mark 10:7–8).

In marriage a man and a woman come together as a unit, and God's ideal is that this oneness be reflected in our parenting style. As a father and mother, we *co*operate, *co*labor, and *co*ordinate. *We are a team.* As one husband wrote to me, marriage is not a competition to see who has the best ideas. "It's a team effort. All for one and one for all." Perhaps the Preacher put it best: "Two are better than one because they have a good return for their labor" (Ecclesiastes 4:9).

Sarah and I had both known pain from the lack of teamwork by our parents. It led to divorce in both of our homes (fortunately, my parents remarried each other), and we were determined to be a cohesive unit. We had each seen firsthand the truth of the motto "United we stand, divided we fall." Our parents fell, and we determined not to let this happen to our marriage and to our children. In my case I had cried myself to sleep many a night as my mom and dad argued and fought. Sarah had experienced the same kind of emotional scarring.

So from the time our kids were very small, Sarah and I recognized the wisdom in parental teamwork and focused on unity. Did Sarah and I always agree? No, but we distinguished unity (a united and harmonious front) from unanimity (having to absolutely agree all the time on all aspects). We subscribed to the belief that if we always agreed, one of us was unnecessary. Often we would debate opposing opinions and ideas about the children behind closed doors. Sometimes the sparks flew, but we knew God had made us male and female to spark better ideas and insight. To slightly paraphrase Proverbs 27:17: "Iron sharpens iron, so one spouse sharpens another." We were confident our differences led to better decisions.

*I pray that all of these people continue to have unity in the way that you, Father, are in me and I am in you. I pray that they may be united with us so that the world will believe that you have sent me.*

*—John 17:21 GW*

When we came out to face our kids, they knew they could not divide Mom and Dad and conquer by getting their way. Our adult kids are proof that children are tuned in to how their parents handle these situations. Now a parent himself, Jonathan looks back and reflects on our solidarity, noting that Mom and Dad "always waited and made decisions as a team." And Joy recalls, "You guys did great teamwork. We knew that 'divide and conquer' was not going to work, no matter how much we tried to work you."

Another passage that inspired our unity was Mark 3:25: "If a house is divided against itself, that house will not be able to stand." We must work at being allies, or we could end up as enemies. As Eugene Peterson puts it in *The Message*, "A constantly squabbling family disintegrates."

One wife wrote to me of their parenting challenges: "I just want us as a couple to be a team. I know he desires this, too, but I think we both need to take some steps in order for this to happen." I agree and recommend three steps.

## Put Your Marriage First, Your Children Second

This idea may sound radical, but I believe it is the best way to ensure God's best for your children. A woman who is in her sec-

> *She is your companion, the wife of your marriage vows.*
>
> —*Malachi 2:14* GW

ond separation from her husband wrote, "I felt no commitment, no partnership . . . I never felt he set our marriage apart from the family unit or that it was the most important relationship (other than relationship with God)."

We never serve our children well when we serve each other divorce papers.[1] Often parents tell me: "I love my children and really don't want to hurt them or screw them up. I know how my parents' divorce affected me. I never want to break my sweet children's hearts . . ."

I agree. For this reason, working together to have a truly loving and respectful team is imperative. Displaying animosity and divisiveness creates emotional havoc in the child. Grown children from divisive, separated, or divorced homes are often depressed and find it hard to trust in building marital relationships of their own. Both a legal divorce and an emotional divorce hurt the children—they break our sweet children's hearts.

Enough of the negative. How do we seek the positive? We can begin by taking a moment to renew our commitment to our marriage vows, which means we must go back and start with our commitment to God Himself. The final session of a Love & Respect conference emphasizes the Rewarded Cycle: his love regardless of her respect . . . her respect regardless of his love. We do our marriage (and our parenting) as unto Christ. As one spouse wrote after attending the conference, "I cried; I wept like a baby, especially at the end, when I learned that how we treat our spouse is how we treat our beloved Lord and Savior . . . I am on a mission to break the curse that has been destroying our family for years."

Another letter from a husband commented, "I keep watching the Rewarded Cycle for encouragement, to love her no matter what and realize it's not about my wife but my relationship to God. We have two teens. It has been rough, but I realize my role and how I've been selfish and looking only to my needs, instead of providing for her needs."

The right order is God first, then our marriage, then our kids. When we have this straight, good things happen in the hearts of our children. This is not rocket science; it is a human love and respect relationship as God intended. Children feel far more loved when they know their parents love and respect each other first and foremost. As one mom put it, "Our children have giggled, watching us kiss, hug, play, and be a mommy and daddy who love each other and them. Taking a minute here and there to love each other brings smiles to their faces I didn't expect. They love us loving each other!"

When our kids were younger, they sometimes would smart off to Sarah, and I would say: "Quit talking to Mom that way. She is my girlfriend. When you grow up, you will leave our home, but she and I are staying together. In fact, when you leave, she and I are going to party. So stop talking disrespectfully to my woman."

When I asked our kids as adults what they recall of that comment, David said, "I thought it was great. I wanted you to party . . . you never had before." Joy concurred. "I thought, *There's no way they are going to party!*"

Okay, so maybe they missed my point a bit. I was trying to say, "We are a team first and foremost, so don't mess with my gal, and oh, by the way, feel secure and safe because of this." Joy did add: "You and Mom dancing around the kitchen was always something we would watch . . . Isn't there research on kids feeling safer when their parents are affectionate? If not, I still think it's definitely true. You can quote me as the on-the-spot researcher."

Obviously when I speak of husband-wife togetherness, I am not justifying parents who habitually leave their kids with babysitters and pursue self-centered pleasure just for themselves. But I do want to challenge and caution parents who may be fixating on their kids at the expense of their marriage. It is possible to unthinkingly put your kids on a pedestal, like idols. And when we worship our kids, we desecrate them. While I do not think Sarah and I ever fell into that trap, I do recall saying once when the kids were younger, "Do you think we can get together, just the two of us, and not talk about the kids—at least for a little while?"

Sarah remembers this comment as a revelation. Up until then, she had never believed she was overlooking our relationship by giving the daily report about the children. She always felt energized by these discussions. Isn't that what mothers and fathers are supposed to do? But what I said made her think, *Oh my. He does have his own life and wants to spend some of that with me. He wants alone time, just with me. The kids will grow up and leave, and we will remain behind. We need to keep the marriage fires burning.*

In Sarah's words I hear a gentle warning: we must never conclude that we have to choose between parenting and marriage. We do not put the marriage on hold until the kids grow up and leave. God's design is a family structure with two roles: spouse and parent. The encumbrances and inconveniences of trying to do marriage and parenting are taxing, but possible in His strength.

The crux of the issue is this: the best thing a father can do for his children is love God and their mother, and the best thing a mother can do for her children is reverence God and respect their father.[2]

# Believe in Each Other's Goodwill

Whatever their differences, most spouses have goodwill toward each other. By goodwill I mean "the deep-down intention to do good toward the other." Granted, we do not always follow through. In the Garden of Gethsemane, when Jesus went to pray, three of His disciples who were to keep watch fell asleep. Our Lord said to them, "The spirit is willing, but the flesh is weak" (Matthew 26:41). The apostle Paul also captured the reality of good intentions but poor follow-through when he wrote of his own struggles with the flesh in Romans 7:19: "I want to do what is good, but I don't. I don't want to do what is wrong, but I do it anyway" (NLT). We all know what Paul is talking about. You or your spouse may want to do the right thing, but you don't; or you or your spouse may want to stop doing the wrong things, but you don't. When your spouse fails to follow through on his or her good intentions, your definition of goodwill must include the idea that goodwilled people do not mean any harm. They do not intend real evil toward one another.

But in the daily give-and-take of marriage and the stress of parenting, it is easy to start thinking your spouse does not have your best interests at heart. Your spouse may be neglectful, forgetful, careless, or hurtful, and as a result you become hurt or angry enough to lash out in return. The chronic stress and negativity pull you both under, and you doubt each other's goodwill. Spouses need a reminder to give each other the benefit of the doubt.

*Neither intend to displease the other, as the Bible says, "one who is married is concerned about the things of the world, how he may please his wife, and . . . how she may please her husband"* (1 Corinthians 7:33–34).

Often I have asked couples during counseling, "Is your spouse a goodwilled person?" Both readily answer, "Yes." Many couples have told me that this question revolutionized their marriage. To acknowledge that deep down they know their spouse has goodwill despite all the stuff that might be going on puts them on a positive path to teamwork, even though they may still have strong differences and irritations.

Trust the goodwill in your spouse, if for no other reason than the sake of your kids. How sad when children see the basic goodwill in mom and dad, but mom and dad do not see this basic goodwill in each other.

I am often asked how I reconcile goodwill with human depravity. Every part of our being is infected by sin, just as dye permeates every drop of a glass of water. But—and it is a big *but*—we are made in the image of God and can act accordingly with goodwill. We can desire to do what is right and do it to some degree.[3] It is recognizing this desire in a spouse that can create teamwork. While husbands or wives may be thoughtless and unpleasant on occasion, it is best not to believe they have wicked motives. They are simply human. They may know Christ, but they do not always do what they know they should (Romans 7:19).

As you seek to work as a team, there will be many stresses and irritations that come up in the flow of daily living together. Many times a mother is weighed down by her burdens for the kids. At those moments she can sound critical, even disrespectful. Let me caution all husbands: she is not using the kids as a pretext to send you messages of disapproval and disrespect. When your wife complains, give her the benefit of the doubt. She is not trying to be a nagger and a critic. She longs to work as a team. When you withdraw because you think she is putting you down, you fail to see her need for your strength and support. Decode her goodwill and good heart. She cares. Don't personalize this as an attack on you.

Sometimes, however, a wife can err in how she expresses her negative feelings. In one family the husband proposed having a Bible study with the children, but his wife nixed the idea right in front of everyone. She said it would take too long and could be boring for children. It turned out she was simply trying to protect them from her husband's tendency to be long-winded with his rather extreme views of what Scripture meant. Unfortunately, she missed an opportunity to support and encourage her husband's goodwilled intentions to lead the family spiritually.

What might she have done differently? She could have kept her silence when he proposed the idea, then privately suggested having shorter passages of Scripture and limiting the time to what was age appropriate for the kids. As best as a wife can, she needs to give her husband the benefit of the doubt, trusting his goodwill, especially when he tries to do the right thing.

## A Case Study in Parents Showing Each Other Goodwill

Following is an example of how a couple—Jim and Cathie—

assumed goodwill in each other in spite of serious parental issues, though they never used the term. The husband wrote to tell me of how they had been practicing the art of love and respect for over a year when their nineteen-year-old daughter returned home from a five-month short-term mission trip. Before she left, they had agreed that on her return they would urge her to enroll in college, to keep her insurance coverage intact. If she chose not to go to college, she would have to work full-time and provide her own insurance. The girl had been home but a few days when Cathie casually mentioned that if their daughter "needed a dental cleaning or something else, we would take care of it." Jim thought this did not sound like their agreement and said so. The Crazy Cycle cranked up, and then "everything fell apart." Cathie felt Jim was being unloving, and he felt she had ignored their agreement and was telling him what they were going to do.

Cathie felt unloved, Jim felt disrespected, and they moved into their "old dance." Because she had apparently disregarded his opinions, he tried to stonewall her, not wanting to get into a battle of words where "she can trounce me every time." But she kept after him, and he realized he had to make the first move and share his heart, hard as that was for him, a typical male. He explained he cared for their daughter, but it felt like Cathie was making decisions contrary to what they had decided, going over his head, rather than working with him. Jim stressed that he loved them both and did not want to get between his wife and her "mother bear" need to protect their daughter.

Cathie responded that she did not intend to take control. They kissed and left for their respective jobs. "I was trying to practice love," he wrote, "but in reality still didn't feel respected. I was hoping that with time my mood would change and I'd just begrudgingly give in."

Jim felt he had done his part to mend the rift, but admits "the real effort came from her later." He was in the midst of an awful day with failing equipment and people wanting attention when she called to check in. He voiced his frustration with all the problems, and she softly tried to encourage him. Just then another call came in, and he switched to another line as she supposedly hung up. A few minutes later the other call ended, and as he holstered his cell phone he could hear a voice. It was Cathie, praying with conviction for him. Somehow her call had not disconnected. She had been praying for him the whole time.

Jim concluded his letter by saying he was not sure if everything came together that day, but it had started with his wife seeming not to respect his wishes, and it ended with her shattering his bad mood and pumping him "full of confidence and respect. I caught her respecting my socks off . . . She knows the secret of respect, and I'm starting to come around myself."

What a great story of goodwill in action. They had an issue. They came close to failing to see each other's true heart. How easy it would have been for her to have felt hurt and unloved and for him to misconstrue her as disrespectful. But the unusual circumstances, as Jim overheard Cathie praying for him over the phone, caused him to see clearly Cathie's goodwill toward him. What a privileged moment for him.

I share this letter and its story as a visual aid to remind us that we need to trust the goodwill in our mate, even if we don't always see it as clearly as Jim saw it that day. Otherwise, teamwork can be undermined during sharp disagreements because we imagine our spouse has ill will. To be a true parental team, the loving and respectful thing to do is to refrain from labeling your partner as mean-spirited. And that brings us to step three.

# Speak with Love and Respect

I often get letters from wives who say they need respect just as much as a man. Absolutely. We all need love and respect equally.

*Each one of you also must love his wife as he loves himself, and the wife must respect her husband.*

*—Ephesians 5:33 NIV*

In my book *Love & Respect*, I talk about a woman's desire for esteem from her husband, which is his loving way of respecting her. A man cannot honestly tell a woman, "I love you" if he does not esteem and respect her.

On the other hand, as much as women need respect, when it comes to deeper issues of the heart, you can bet your last dollar they will revolve around love. No movie ends with the guy embracing his woman and saying, "I respect you with all my heart!" In fact, we asked seven thousand people, "When you are in a conflict with your significant other, do you feel unloved at that moment or disrespected?" Seventy-two percent of the women feel unloved, whereas 83 percent of the men feel disrespected.

Research by Shaunti Feldhahn, reported in her classic book *For Women Only*, has clearly shown that if asked which would be worse—to be left alone and unloved, or to be viewed as inadequate and disrespected—80 percent of the men cannot stand the idea of being viewed as inadequate and disrespected.[4]

Generally speaking, if you want teamwork in parenting, be sure your wife hears you speaking with loving tones and words and your husband hears respectful tones and words.

A surefire way to ignite teamwork with a wife is to praise her heart for mothering. Years ago, when all three of our kids were small, I told Sarah one day, "If I had your job, I'd be in prison!" Later she commented, "That made me so happy! Not that you'd be in prison, but that you understood how hard mothering could be. I felt so loved and esteemed."

The truth is, as our children have grown to adulthood, I clearly credit most everything to Sarah's mothering. Though I am committed to fathering, she is consumed with mothering. She is head and shoulders above me as a parent.

A wife is naturally equipped with a nurturing nature and quickly zeros in on what upsets her child. It is the wise husband who lets his wife advise and guide in these situations. He does not react negatively to her suggestions. A man who lovingly receives his wife's reports, contributions, and even her complaints will see her become inspired and excited about their relationship and teamwork as parents. But if he takes offense over what he thinks is condescension toward him, he will fail to esteem her loving heart and foil their teamwork.

But love and respect work both ways. It is a wise woman who realizes the importance of listening to her husband's opinions, rather than subtly discounting or ignoring them. This can happen so easily in parenting situations because wives are so nurturing and loving of their families they may not realize they are being perceived as disrespectful by their husbands.

When does a man feel disrespected in the family? In a couples' Bible study focused on Love & Respect, the wives wanted to know what made men feel disrespected at home. A significant reason stood out: "When my wife does not value my input on family affairs."

Following is a letter from a wife who was facing serious tension with her husband because of their daughter's impending wedding and how much it was going to cost. There had been little clear discussion about who was paying for what, and the husband was feeling that everyone just ignored what he thought and no one was showing him any respect. Whenever he brought the expenses up to his wife, she had a tendency to think he just went on and on and that caused her to zone out or get defensive. Her usual response was, "She's my only child, my only daughter, and I want her to have a nice wedding," which only increased the tension. Finally, she realized this was not working and decided to practice respect. She wrote:

> I looked at it from his standpoint and agreed with everything he was saying and apologized and told him I was wrong for how I was handling it . . . I explained my position of being in the middle, between the two of them . . . We talked over the wedding budget and agreed on how much we would contribute. He settled right down, and we were able to discuss it clearly and rationally without it turning into a war. In the past, I would try to get him to settle down by telling him I loved him, and he would say, "I know that! But you take me for granted!" He doesn't use the "respect" word, but he does use "taken for granted." . . . I never understood why telling him of my love wasn't enough. After it was over, we were closer . . . it felt like we were a *team working together* on the problem.

A team! She gets it! She realized she had appeared disrespectful and made the adjustment. So many wives do not intend to be disrespectful, but they do not understand their husbands are "blue" while they are "pink." Husbands are good-willed, but they see, think, and feel differently from women about many things. With wedding excitement mounting, this wife's pink worldview consumed her as she anticipated the joy in her soon-to-be-married daughter. She had been zoning out or getting defensive because she simply could not grasp why he couldn't change his "spoiled, childish attitude" about money and simply go along and enjoy the entire experience as she planned to do.

The answer was simple, and fortunately she finally saw it. Her husband was not spoiled and childish; his blue view of the whole thing was simply different from her pink one. He was not wrong, just different, and his repeated charge, "You take me for granted," finally got through to her. They were able to stop the Crazy Cycle and work it out. Once he knew he was being heard and not taken for granted, they could come together and work on what concerned him most: a budget.

Men have strengths and vulnerabilities where wives do not, and wives have strengths and vulnerabilities their husbands do not. If they hope to build a team, they must work together with unconditional love and respect.[5] They must blend her pink and his blue to make God's purple, two becoming one—a team committed to doing their marriage as unto Christ.[6]

God designed us to have two views. Instead of trying to prove your mate wrong with a win-lose approach, learn to disagree agreeably with goodwill and come to a win-win solution. Because I disagree at times with Sarah does not make her wrong and me right. We subscribe to a simple axiom: not wrong, just different. Then we move ahead to blend our opinions for the good of the team, and most importantly, the rest of the family.

Ecclesiastes 4:9 says two are better than one, but also note the wisdom in verses 10–12: "If one person falls, the other can reach out and help. But someone who falls alone is in real trouble. Likewise, two people lying close together can keep each other warm. But how can one be warm alone? A person standing alone can be attacked and defeated, but two can stand back-to-back and conquer" (NLT).

I cannot answer who is right when you and your spouse differ. I can say with conviction that your children will suffer the consequences long-term if the two of you cannot come together to put God and each other first. Believe in each other's goodwill, act and speak with love and respect, and blend your pink and blue views into the heavenly royal color of purple.

*Pink and blue—not wrong, just different.* This could be as important as any other principle in the Love & Respect design for your family. It is so important that there is still much more to learn about pink and blue and how to parent your children according to their gender. Boys and girls need different approaches, as the next chapter will explain.

———

For more information on the following topics, go to
www.loveandrespect.com/parent/teamwork:

- Should parents ever divorce for the sake of the children?
- How to see goodwill in your spouse—no matter what

# 11

# PARENTING PINK AND BLUE

For me this is one of the most intriguing chapters in the entire book because of my fascination with the way God made us as male and female. Maleness and femaleness manifest themselves early. A child of the opposite sex can appear like a foreigner. One parent quipped, "We love these kids, but Lord help us; if they don't have the same XX or XY chromosomes that we do, it can be like navigating through a foreign country without a map."

I think I discovered foundational information related to love and respect that explains these male and female chromosomes and helps us parent pink and blue kids who are equal but not the same. Genetically, we know that boys and girls are different.[1] It is critical that parents pay attention to these pink and blue distinctions in their children, which are rooted in God's design of male and female (Matthew 19:4). Abundant research confirms God's creative handiwork. For example, girls need to be liked and socially connected; boys need to be respected.[2] My friend Shaunti Feldhahn, a great researcher, found an undeniable pattern when researching her book *For Parents Only*: girls lean toward the need to feel loved, and boys lean toward the need to be respected.[3]

Unfortunately, in my opinion, some researchers do not interpret boys correctly. For example, preschool girls alternate taking turns with others twenty times more often than boys. Boys are twenty times more aggressive in taking action and competing with others without concern of conflict, and when at play they strongly defend their territory.[4] For not a few researchers, these findings make girls caring and boys hyper . . . even violent. This same information, however, could be interpreted to say boys like to develop their abilities to aggressively defend and protect the innocent with little concern for their very lives, particularly if the conflict is between good and evil.

I have a friend who has a restaurant that caters to preschool and early elementary boys and girls. He created a Princess Room in one part of the facility. When the boys and girls enter the room, the girls fall all over themselves to put on the dresses, wear the crowns, walk in the heels, and wave the wands. They long to be that special and beloved princess. The boys, though, show no such interest in the Princess Room. But as the boys turn to leave, they see the plastic swords lined up on the entrance wall. Whoa! They pick up the swords and the fun begins.

*But in the beginning, at the time of creation, "God made them male and female," as the scripture says (Mark 10:6 GNT).*

*Boys are not wrong for being boys but simply different from girls. God made them this way.*

Some people, often mothers, feel uncomfortable with the fact that boys go for the weapons. My interpretation is that their sons envision themselves honorably defending the fort against an evil intruder (and later lovingly protecting the damsel in distress). No boy can fully give voice to this sentiment, but it is in his genes. We need to see these young lads as seeking to be noble, not as potentially violent, intent on hurting others.

We need to see children as goodwilled but different, equal but not the same. A teen girl looks at life through her pink lenses related to matters of love, and a teen boy gazes through his blue lenses related to matters of respect. We sanction the girl's need for love, but we tend to see the boy's need for respect as arrogant.

As believers we need to recognize God's design. As boys and girls become men and women who marry, they will need to apply Ephesians 5:33. There we learn that a wife needs to feel loved regardless of her lovability and a husband needs to feel respected for who he is deep in his heart even though he fails to be respectable all the time and in every way. This principle is as important for parenting as it is for marriage. We need to understand why our sons and daughters deflate and react when they feel disrespected and unloved. *The man is in the boy, and the woman is in the girl.* Neither is wrong, just different.

What do I mean by loving girls and respecting boys? What I do *not* mean is that girls do not need respect and boys do not need love. More on that later, but for now I invite you to look with me at two crucial relationships that can revolutionize how you parent your children.

## The Mother-Son Relationship: Her Respect

Mothers continually tell me how using the respect message has led to a whole new level of meaningful connection with their sons. After attending our marriage conference, one mom wrote to tell me she had decided to start using respect talk with her son:

When my son gives me his insights, I say, "I really respect what you have to say," or "I respect the way you handled that situation," or "I really respect how you are taking initiative to get things done and follow through." This has made my son smile like I have never seen. I talk more about respect regarding sporting events and showing respect for your opponent. My son always knew I loved him. Now he knows that I respect him and his ideas, something I didn't do so well in the past.

*Males possess virtues worthy of imitation. For example, all of us are to "act like men, be strong" (1 Corinthians 16:13). Mothers can honor such qualities in their sons.*

Another mother reported a conversation she had with her seven-year-old son that is a classic demonstration of the power of showing respect to a male.

MOM: I respect you.

SON: (half of a charitable grin)

MOM: Do you know what that means?

SON: (quick side-to-side shake of head, meaning no)

MOM: Well, it means I'm proud of you, and I think you're honorable, and I think you're a strong man.

SON: (sitting up straighter with sheepish grin) Thanks, Mom.

MOM: Which do you like to hear more? That I'm proud of you and think you are a strong man, or that I love you?

SON: Proud and strong.

Her seven-year-old knows she loves him, but respect is something new, and he loves that!

Respect talk works with male children, no matter their age, but when I say "respect talk works" I do not mean manipulating him or getting him to perform a certain way. Respect talk works with your son because it meets the ingrained need for respect deep in his spirit. Yes, you love him, but the best way to communicate your love is to show respect to the very spirit of your son, a spirit precious to God. He will sometimes fail to be who he ought to be, but he still needs respect. You may not always feel that he deserves your respect, but it is during those moments he needs it the most.

Following are three tested ways for mothers to speak and act respect with their sons.

## Pay Attention to What They Are Saying

A mother shared about her nine-year-old son: "I received the cutest handwritten Mother's Day card this week, and you would be amazed what the first line of the card said: 'I appreciate you because you are respectful.' The rest of the card talked about being thankful for doing his laundry and how I am good at math, but the 'respect' comment was on the top."

And listen to this mom's testimony:

One night while putting our sons to bed, my five-year-old, in the midst of my monologue about how much I loved him, looked at me sadly and said, "Mom, are you proud of me?" Shocked, I expressed immediately that I was, of course, proud of him. He asked forlornly, "Then why don't you ever tell me so?" Ever since then, I have worked to hold back on my desire to grab him up off the floor and smother his cheek with kisses, and instead, I practice putting one hand on his shoulder and telling him I'm proud of him. He responds to that simple gesture by puffing out his chest and replying, "Thanks, Mom," with a nod of his head. And he walks away feeling more valued than if I'd kissed his cheek for a year.

Boys are crying out for respect, if only moms would listen carefully to what they are saying. One mother wrote:

> I have found with my boys that anger and control enraged them and bottom line they felt disrespected. At such an early age I can see that this is what they have asked of me. When I am encouraging, patient, accepting of their mistakes, and gentle in correction and building them up in character, I have a much more peaceful home . . . I am trying to not tear my house down with my tongue!

This mom "gets it," and she sets up our next point.

## Just Be with Them . . . and Talk Less!

Being shoulder to shoulder with their husbands and not talking to them is a revelation to many wives at our conferences. It also works with sons. A mother wrote of how she could see her puberty-age boys needed a different approach: the lullabies had stopped; their need for comfort when hurt physically was much less; the sense that they "belonged to her" was fading. She recalled reading in a James Dobson book that talking with boys while doing some task could be effective, so she decided one day to let them watch as she baked cookies.

She didn't ask them to help; she just

*We must not lose sight of common sense when it comes to male and female. "Ask around! Look around! Can men bear babies?" (Jeremiah 30:6 MSG).*

started mixing cookie dough, being careful to say little or nothing. Eventually they wanted to join in. As they worked together, rolling cookie dough in cinnamon sugar, she learned what was on their minds. They were soon talking about the family, what her mother had done while she was growing up, their dreams—even what was happening at school.

After taking ten dozen cookies out of the oven, they all had some together. She closed her letter: "It was a rewarding afternoon and a great time to reconnect. This was the same evening my soon-to-be twelve-year-old asked to be tucked in! He must have felt the same things I was feeling. All because I took the time to slow down and let him just be."

Did you catch that? *The twelve-year-old* wanted mom to tuck him in. Shoulder-to-shoulder activities with boys can ignite their affection and love for mom even during puberty when affection seems to be fading away.

I often hear from mothers who ask too many questions of their sons. One mom came home to quiz her four-year-old on how things had gone with the sitter:

"Did you play games?"

"Yes, Mom."

"What were they?"

"Hiding games."

"What did you hide?"

"Toys."

"What kind of toys?"

"My toys."

"Did Sissy play too?"

"Yes, Mom."

"Did you find all of the toys?"

"Yes, Mom . . . can we please stop talking now?"

This typical mom with typical questions learned her typical little guy was not really interested in what to him was ancient history. This disinterest and even dislike for questions continues as boys grow older. (See Sarah's "How was school?" experience with David in chapter 5, page 61.)

In many cases when moms talk less, their sons talk more. There are, of course, times when mom *should* talk, especially to . . .

## Speak Respect to Your Son

You can't just think about being more respectful to your son; you must constantly speak respect, which I assure you he will appreciate much more than questions. A mom shared:

> I'm still amazed how just using the words *respect*, *appreciate*, or *admire* seem to make a great difference with my husband and sons. I look forward to what the Lord has in store for my family. I am being continually challenged to be respectful and to choose respectful words. It is difficult after trying to protect myself with the wrong words.

Another mom told me:

> When addressing my son, I make sure that he knows how important respect is when dealing with everyone. I also make sure that he knows how much I value and respect his feelings, as well as the fact that he is willing to share those feelings. I've learned that even though he is "only eleven," I still have to show him respect. I choose my words carefully. I never want him to feel belittled. I am always watchful that my words do not crush his spirit.

Mom, be aware that you can crush your son's spirit not only with words but also with the look on your face and your tone of voice, even when you think you are "just trying to help him learn." Many mothers feel so much love for their sons that it blinds them to the need the boy has for respect. She assumes that he should know the depth of her love. But she must recognize that though she loves him, she can appear to be disgusted with him. For example, in correcting him, she can appear condescending.

One mom wrote:

> Until recently, when I would discipline my oldest, I would talk "down" to him . . . did this work? Obviously not. I was frustrated and had been praying for an answer on how to understand my son and his needs as a young man. Well, they are not very different from my husband's. He appreciates respect, and his response has been positive and less frustrating to me.

This truth came home to a mother of a fifteen-year-old boy who left her stunned, shocked, and amazed. She shared:

> My son has started a new control technique with me lately. He felt he could yell loudly his opinions, at the top of his voice, then expect me to see things his way and accept it as being so. He tried this with going places with friends and with buying things, to name a couple. I used to express calmly to him that the last I recalled, I'm the parent and he's the child, not the other way around. I tried to give suggestions on how to talk about things with me so I would be more responsive to his ideas. Things just ended in a big verbal battle. He felt horrible, and I did too. During his latest outbursts of demands, all I said

was, "I respect how you've come to ask something of me, and I want to hear what you're saying to make a good decision. I can't seem to get past the loudness . . . it feels very unloving." He normally would have continued his yelling, no matter how I responded to him, but this time he was taken back a bit and went to his room. Then he came back, and we actually talked out his plans. I was slightly in a state of shock and euphoria at the same time.

She spoke one word that differed from all other times she appealed to her son. That word was *respect*.

A mom of adult sons wrote:

In talking to my sons on the phone, instead of always ending our conversation with "I love you," I said, "I respect . . . (made it personal to their situation)." One son got quiet and then said, "Thank you, Mom," which really touched my heart. Another son who is more distant from us emotionally and spiritually also got quiet and then said, "I love you," which he seldom says to me. That was awesome.

The application of respect talk to sons is leaving mothers overwhelmed with joy. Though this is no formula, it leads to more frequent connections with sons.

Every mother says that she respects her baby boy. Why else would she confront him and want mutual understanding and connection with him? But she needs to step back and observe how she talks to her son. Not a few mothers appear to their sons as being mad at them. Boys translate that through the respect grid and close off. Whereas a daughter is more likely to understand that mom is frustrated, boys do not discern this as well.

Also, because a boy does not break down and cry like a daughter might, a mom can feel her son is growing hard against her, so she ups her words of disapproval. Instead of softening, he pulls back his heart even more. When a mom discerns how negative she seems and makes an adjustment, her relationship with her boy changes for the better.

One woman wrote: "I am making a point of praising and respecting my husband in front of our sons, and all four of them are standing taller!" There is much more to learn about pink and blue differences between mothers and their sons. For more tips, insights, and suggestions, go to www.loveandrespect.com /parenting/gender.

## The Father-Daughter Relationship: His Love

That a father ought to love his daughter in a special way is not new information. Unlike a lot of moms who may not be aware of the need to speak respectfully to their sons, most dads know of a daughter's need for dad's love because their wives coach them.

Why does mom coach dad in this way? Because she hopes he will do toward the daughter what was meaningful for her as a little girl and what is still meaningful to her today.

You may have heard that "the best way to love your daughter is to love her mother." That is excellent advice. If a daughter constantly sees her parents on the Crazy Cycle, she may start to believe that her dad does not love her either.

*Isaiah captures the emotional pain a young woman feels when rejected. She feels "forsaken and grieved" (54:6a), "a woman hated from her youth" (54:6b BRENTON).*

A key trait dads must understand about daughters—and women—is that they tend to personalize what is said to them and, probably more important, how it is said. If you have to confront or correct your daughter, try to do it gently. No father ever intends to reject his daughter, but when dad seems to be chastising her, she may easily think he is saying, "I really don't love you." We dads need to ask ourselves, "When I confront or correct my daughter, could I be going overboard and causing her to feel unloved and unfairly criticized?"

When she fails, she'll be extremely hard on herself, so be sure to point out the positives and to share that you love how teachable she is. Encourage her to learn from her mistakes, but do not harp on them. That would be a vastly bigger mistake than any she might make.

I often get letters from wives who say they need respect as well as love. Amy, thirteen, concurs, saying she is very secure in her parents' unconditional love, but she also needs respect, and likes to be told by her dad, "Well done." Nonetheless, she went on to say, "But if the question is which one could you not live without (love or respect) . . . without question I could not live without my parents' love. It is more like a need than a want."

Amy's observations on respect versus love say to me that daughters respond first to affirmation of who they are as a person. Daughters appreciate compliments on their performance, but if that is all that dad ever praises them for, then they will intuitively feel that if they do not perform well, they will not be accepted and loved.

Most daughters wonder, *Does Dad love me for me, no matter what?* This is why no more harmful words can be spoken by a dad to his daughter than, "No one could ever love you." It is hard to believe any dad would say this to a daughter, but I have many letters from women telling me this is what happened to them.

As you relate to your daughter, keep in mind that her female brain is "hardwired" with special aptitudes: to be very verbal, to connect deeply in friendships, to defuse conflict, and a "nearly psychic capacity to read faces and tone of voice for emotions and states of mind."[5] God calls dads to understand and work with His precious design. Following are just a few things for dads to remember as they parent their daughters.

### From Infancy On, Females Want to Look You in the Eye

According to research specialists, during the first three months of life a baby girl's skills in eye contact and facial gazing increase by over 400 percent, but there is no such increase in boys. When there is a lack of facial expression, girls become confused and turn away. Infant girls are also more sensitive to human voices than boys. They have a sense of self that is connected to how well they are listened to by adults. In fact, one-year-old girls were observed as more capable of empathy by being more responsive to people who looked sad or hurt.[6]

A mother described her ten-month-old daughter: "Her idea of playing involves me lying flat on my back so she can climb on me, peer down into my face, and press her nose against mine while looking into my eyes, grinning and jabbering with delight."

*As a husband is to be "understanding" of a wife "since she is a woman," the same holds true of a dad toward his daughter—since she is a woman (1 Peter 3:7).*

As daughters grow up and become young women, then wives, their need to look you in the eye continues and matures. Wise is the dad and husband who looks right back.

**Love Is Her Native Language**

Expressions of love run deep in a daughter, and she yearns to hear them early on. Here is an example of a father making his daughter feel she is the apple of his eye. When she was around four, they got into an "I love you more" exchange. Dad had just told his little girl, "I love you all the way around the world and back." Her reply: "I love you all the way on top of God!" His letter continues: "That left me theologically stunned. She had trumped me soundly." Whether a pinkie is four or forty, love is the language she hears best.

How different and sad is a letter from an adult daughter who remembers seeing her "emotionally cold and distant" dad sitting in church twice on Sundays, hearing God's Word, but "I never remember sitting on his lap, him holding my hand, or him ever telling me that he loved me . . . It all was very confusing to me."

**Do Not Ask Them to Stuff Their Feelings**

When our kids were younger, Sarah and I would instruct them, "Cry softly." We were okay with some tears, but not out-of-control weeping and wailing, especially in public. Recently, I asked Joy, "What do you recall about us telling you to cry softly?" Joy replied: "I hated it. Sometimes we were out of line, but I also felt like my crying wasn't validated and that my sadness wasn't acknowledged . . . even though you probably did. I remember hating that 'Cry softly, we are in public' line because crying is something that takes over your body and it's hard to push it back." Joy heard our request to control her crying as, "Stuff your feelings." You can learn from our mistake. I can certainly say that

> *Dads must accept those moments when his daughter is "like hysterical schoolgirls, screaming" (Isaiah 19:16 MSG).*

a dad should never tell his daughter, "Stop crying!" Girls, and their mothers, feel things deeply, and crying is part of how God enables them to release their burdens.

## Decode the Drama with Your Teenage Daughter

A lot of dads would agree that the word *drama* could be printed on the foreheads of some of their teenage daughters. A father needs to recognize that many times his teen daughter erupts with dramatic words of disagreement and protest not because she is trying to be disrespectful toward him as a dad but because she feels secondary. The underlying cause of her "commotion of emotion" is that she needs his reassuring love. She expects her dad to love her in spite of her apparent disrespect.

I think about the dad who makes a date to take his thirteen-year-old to the mall, but something comes up at work, and he has to cancel. He, unfortunately, does not have a lot of time to explain, so he just sends a quick text: "Sorry, Honey . . . maybe next time." But his daughter was counting on this and she angrily texts back: "This ALWAYS happens! You NEVER keep your promises!!!!"

If dad interprets his daughter's dramatic outburst as contempt for who he is, he will withdraw from her emotionally to prevent an escalation of the conflict or blow up in anger at her over-the-top accusations. Either way, he can appear as though he does not care about her, which misrepresents his deepest heart. The daughter really needs his love even though she has reacted immaturely, which can easily seem like disrespect.

If dad sees her disappointment and frustration, they can work it out. But if he harshly tries to "teach her she can't talk that way," she will become only more convinced that she is not the apple of his eye and can have a "daddy wound" that could last a lifetime.

There are many other insights and practical ideas on "pink

and blue" differences between dads and their daughters that could be shared here. For more information go to loveandrespect .com/parenting/gender. You may have questions about two other relationships we did not cover: fathers and sons and mothers and daughters.[7]

## Pink or Blue: She Needs Love, and He Needs Respect

I received a letter from a father who has a son, Matt, a college graduate, and a daughter, Amy, who is working on a degree. He aptly described how love and respect work with daughters and sons.

Amy had been having a tough year, not with studies but with her housemates. When she came home on Christmas break, her dad told her how proud he was of the way she had stuck with the other girls, trying to love them despite what was going on. She appreciated his words but still seemed disturbed and reluctant to go back.

Then Amy talked to her mother, who simply told her they both supported her and loved her "no matter what happened." The lightbulb seemed to go on with a brilliant flash. Amy had been dreading going back for the second semester; now she was totally encouraged and excited. As her dad put it, "It is like our love for her—which she knows she can count on—is a remote force field she can feel safe in. Because she knows we love her and pray for her, she can courageously confront her sisters in Christ."

In the same letter this father described a phone conversation he had with his oldest son, who works for a large parachurch ministry in a distant part of the country. As they talked, he told his son how proud he was of him and how much he respected him. His son asked why, so the father mentioned how he could be making 50 percent more after graduating with highest honors, but he had chosen to use his talents to serve the Lord. This dad went on to mention several other things: how capable his son was in taking care of the car, his consistent service to his church, as well as missionaries he supports. As the dad talked, his son remained quiet on the other end of the phone. The letter continues: "After I had gone through the list of things I had for why I was proud of him, when he spoke, I could tell he was crying. I didn't realize as I was praising him how big a deal it would be for him. It was a lesson to my wife and me. So she sat down and wrote him a letter about why she was proud of him and what she admired about him."

Dad then added that he could see both his grown children still need a lot of support from mom and dad, but the support they need is different. Their son, Matt, "knows we love him, but it doesn't matter that much to him. He needs to know that we are proud of him and admire him. Amy knows we are proud of her, but it doesn't matter that much to her. She needs to know that we love her."

What genders live at your house? Are they getting what they must have?

As we have seen, the Family Crazy Cycle can be decoded and defused. You can use G-U-I-D-E-S to ride the Family Energizing Cycle, but there is one more crucial step for Christ-following parents. The Family Rewarded Cycle is what Christian parenting is really all about, and it has little to do with your kids. We turn there next.

# PART 3

# THE FAMILY REWARDED CYCLE

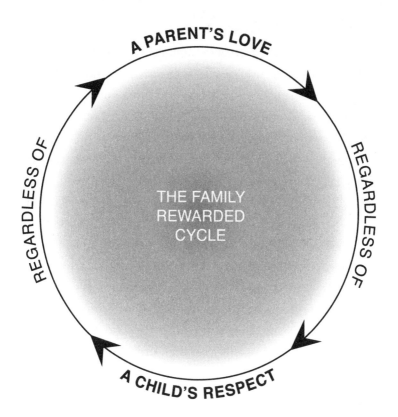

As we have seen, the Family Crazy Cycle spins when children feel unloved and parents feel disrespected. In the Family Energizing Cycle we saw how G-U-I-D-E-S provides a blueprint for parenting God's way and keeping the Family Crazy Cycle in its cage. But what if you try to fully live out G-U-I-D-E-S and your children just are not cooperating?

Though we lovingly Give to our children, they may not always receive from us with gratitude and respect.

Though we lovingly try to Understand our children, they still may become angry or exasperated and accuse us of being unloving.

Though we diligently seek to Instruct our children, they will not always be teachable (sometimes anything but).

Though we attempt to Discipline our children reasonably and fairly, they will at times accuse us of being unfair and unloving.

Though we do our best to Encourage our children, they may still lack courage and confidence at times.

And though we faithfully Supplicate (pray for) our children, there is no ironclad guarantee they will trust and obey God.

No system is foolproof; no blueprint is perfect. That is why the Family Rewarded Cycle is the most important part of how to use Love & Respect in your family. In these chapters you will see that your parenting is more about your relationship with Christ than it is about your relationship with your kids. Here you will learn how to lean completely on the Lord Jesus and never give up . . . never!

# 12

# THE REAL REASON TO
# PARENT GOD'S WAY

## Parenting unto Christ—Our Highest Call

What does this mean for us? The Family Rewarded Cycle visual on page 183 states: "A parent's love regardless of a child's respect . . ." I want to expand on this to say a better statement is "a parent's love unto Jesus Christ and his child, regardless of the child's respect . . ." As parents, we must parent "unto" Jesus Christ regardless of the choices our children make. Parenting God's way means that we parent "unto" Christ even though our child fails to be who we hope he can be.

> As ye have done it unto one of the least of these my brethren, ye have done it unto me.
>
> —*Matthew 25:40 KJV*

How do we "parent unto Christ"? In these Family Rewarded Cycle chapters I hope to show you that I am not talking about ethereal spiritual jargon. To "parent unto Christ" means an entirely different approach. It means to be Christ-conscious in all we do with and for our children—this is God's highest call to parents.

Does the Bible tell us to "parent as unto the Lord"? In Colossians 3:15–24, Paul instructs all believers to be conscious of Christ as present with us in daily living. We are to "let the peace of Christ rule in [our] hearts . . . and be thankful [to God]" (v. 15). We are to "let the word of Christ richly dwell within" us (v. 16). And, whatever we "do in word or deed," we "do all in the name of the Lord Jesus, giving thanks through Him to God the Father" (v. 17).

Briefly put, we are to do what we do and say what we say "as unto the Lord" (for example, Ephesians 5:22 KJV). I prefer the King James translation of "as unto the Lord" or, in some other passages, "as to the Lord" because it is a stronger way to express the idea that all that we do should be done, not just "for" the Lord but "unto" Jesus (Matthew 25:40 KJV). The Lord is actively present. In the total context of Colossians 3:15–24, Paul applies this powerful truth to marriage and family life (especially vv. 18–21). In all of life, and particularly as spouses and parents, we are to rise above horizontal living and be in touch with the vertical relationship we have with our heavenly Father through Jesus Christ our Lord. We are to do what we do "as to the Lord" (v. 23 KJV) because "it is the Lord Christ whom you serve" (v. 24). By the way, in a parallel passage—Ephesians 5:18–6:9—the same truths are set forth. This is no small matter.

To parent "as to the Lord" actually means that in a most profound way this book on parenting has very little to do with children. In a sense, our kids are secondary. This book is not about child-centered parenting but about Christ-centered parenting. Though we are conscious of our children and love them more than our own lives, as we apply G-U-I-D-E-S 24/7, we are to be more conscious of Christ than we are of our children. Beyond the feelings of our children, we are to have a reverent regard for the feelings of Christ, the One we desire to please in the ultimate sense.

In fact, Scripture tells us to love Christ more than we love our kids. Jesus said, "He who loves son or daughter more than Me is not worthy of Me" (Matthew 10:37). Yes, we concentrate on the kids in parenting since that is inescapable, but we focus more on Christ in parenting since that is incomparable.

But if we are to confidently go about our parenting as to the Lord, we must be very clear on who we are in Him. Mentally and emotionally we must seize and hold dear the truth about our eternal value to the Lord. For example, we need to hear the word of Christ concerning our worth. "Look at the birds of the air, that they do not sow, nor reap nor gather into barns, and yet your heavenly Father feeds them. Are you not worth much more than they?" (Matthew 6:26). Each of us must recognize God's forever view of us and the incalculable value He places on us. Most important, does our value to God really affect our marriage and our parenting?

When I weigh the words Jesus used to describe what He has done for me, I am stunned. He has ransomed me, forgiven me, given me eternal life, loved me, and He has prepared a place for me (Matthew 20:28; 26:28; John 3:16; 15:9; 14:2). In letting the word of Christ richly dwell within me, I catch a glimpse of His gracious acceptance, eternal endorsement, and priceless valuation of me. I invite you to comprehend the same—right now. And remember, none of this is merited. We do not earn any of Christ's unwarranted gifts but can only receive them and let all these truths affect the way we parent.

To not understand that our significance and true identity are in Christ and not in our children puts us in danger of being discouraged, as was the mother who wrote,

One of my problems is that when the kids misbehave or don't act as I think they should, then I feel it is such a reflection on me and an extension of me. I suppose it is a pride thing or part of my personality, but do you have any suggestions because this seems to be what wears me down and then paralyzes me, and I feel defeated. Does this make sense?

Her comments make perfect sense to Sarah and me. We have been there. Sarah recalls our very first year of parenting: "I wanted Jonathan to be perfect in the nursery at church. Sadly, he wasn't perfect at three months old, and he cried every Sunday, and I felt like a failure."

As funny as this nursery episode sounds now, it is symbolic of what we felt as parents as the years went on and the matters became more serious. As our children grew, they did what children do—acted imperfectly. Our motive for wanting perfectly behaved children was pure (we wanted to protect them from the consequences of bad choices), but when their behavior caused us to question our worth as parents and even our worth as Christians, we became deeply discouraged. On the heels of many wrong choices made by our children, Sarah and I sat sadly and quietly as we wondered where we had gone wrong. How did we fail to help our children make the right choices? What was wrong with us as parents? Why couldn't we guide them better during their testing and temptations?

There were some dark evenings when we had to deal with these woeful feelings, as many parents must. Would we let these situations conquer us and cause us to stop parenting God's way, as we wallowed in self-pity? The good news is that such reflection put us in a position not only to look for ways to improve our parenting but, more importantly, to face off with our identity in Christ. As we confessed our failures and defects to God, we allowed Him to remind us of His love, that He is for us, and that He will work all things together for our good.

If we allowed our kids' unruliness, irresponsibility, and sinfulness—all "normal" behavior that we were trying to correct—to define our true identity . . .

- our sense of self-worth would go up and down based on how "good" our kids were at all times. For us to feel good about ourselves, our children had to perform well. Obviously this was not fair to us—and certainly not to them.
- we would be making them responsible for our sense of peace, instead of letting the peace of Christ rule in our hearts.
- we would be letting their words about us determine how we felt about ourselves, instead of trusting the words of Christ to determine our sense of self-worth.

As the days passed, Sarah and I humbly let the Scriptures create a new script in our hearts and minds, and so must you. What is your inner script? Have you come to grips with your position in Christ? Do you realize that you have worth because He says you have worth, not because of anything you (or your kids) do or do not do?

As I talk to parents across the country, I find a lot of people who feel defeated as parents because of how their kids behave (or have turned out). What I am about to share with you will not only refresh your soul personally but also enable you to

> *Do not conform yourselves to the standards of this world, but let God transform you inwardly by a complete change of your mind.*
>
> —Romans 12:2 GNT

parent as God intends—or at least make better progress in that direction.

## You Are "Worth Jesus to God"

All of us who believe in Christ as Savior have a "passport to heaven" so to speak, which says, "Because of Jesus Christ, this is a forgiven, accepted, approved, made righteous, made perfect, adopted child of God." As Jesus is *the* Son of God, we are adopted sons and daughters of God. We are in God's family never to be forsaken. This is our true identity. We are beloved children of God—children for whom He has never-ending feelings of compassion. Will we believe that God feels this way about us even when we do not feel this way about ourselves? We must! This is what faith means.

Do you get this? Do you comprehend what it means to be "beloved by God," a refrain used dozens of times in the Bible about all believers? It took Sarah and me some time at first to grasp this truth (and we are still in process to some degree), but when we did, it tremendously affected the way we parented. God's truth was there for the dark moments. We had to accept and believe what all Christian parents must believe: we are worth Jesus to God! The Bible declares: "For you have been bought with a price" (1 Corinthians 6:20; 7:23). What price? "You were not redeemed with perishable things like silver or gold . . . but with precious blood, as of a lamb unblemished and spotless, the blood of Christ" (1 Peter 1:18–19). We were bought with the blood of Christ. His life for our life.

Please join Sarah and me in saying: "Yes, I *am* worth Jesus to God. When God says I have worth, *I have worth!*"

I am well aware that in the daily grind of life, our feelings counter and undermine our trust in our true worth to God. But once we know our worth to God, we cease trying to derive our worth from our children. Yes, today they give us reasons to rejoice and tomorrow they may cause heartache and sorrow, but at no time do they determine our value and importance as redeemed human beings. As believers in Christ we bring our identity to our parenting; we do not derive our identity from our parenting.

As one mother told me, "Our children can't heal our wounds; only God can." She realized how unhealthy her attitude toward her kids was when she expected them to create a healthy self-image in her. She realized she had been trying to hold them accountable for her well-being. She had been requiring them to act obediently to shore up her sagging self-esteem.

One more biblical promise confirms that we are worth Jesus to the Father: our eternal inheritance. "Therefore you are no longer a slave, but a son; and if a son, then an heir through God" (Galatians 4:7). But what does "heir" mean? "The Spirit Himself testifies with our spirit that we are children of God, and if children, heirs also, heirs of God and fellow heirs with Christ" (Romans 8:16–17). There it is! "Fellow heirs with Christ"! "All things belong to [us], and [we] belong to Christ; and Christ belongs to God" (1 Corinthians 3:22b–23).

I have given you this short course on the believer's worth in the eyes of Abba Father to demonstrate that Christian parents have a living, divine document—the oracles of God—that tells us who we are in His eyes (Hebrews 5:12). As we work at parenting each day, we must believe God's truth, even when we do not necessarily feel it.

We must believe that a biblical self-image gives Christian parents a controlling peace during the daily trials—a very practical benefit to us and our kids. So when the dog chews the corner of the couch, our toddler falls down the stairs and breaks an arm, or our teen wrecks the car, we can walk with the assurance of knowing that somehow in only His sovereign wisdom God is always working all this together for the good of those who love Him (*memorize* Romans 8:28). No, we do not expect perfect peace all the time; there will be frustrating and fatiguing days.

> *"Behold, I am coming quickly, and My reward is with Me, to render to every man according to what he has done."*
> —Revelation 22:12

However, if we but ask, moments of God's peace will soften the sharp edges that may form on our demeanor, which could cut and damage our children.

We parent as unto Christ because of our identity in Him, but we also parent unto Jesus for one more reason. An eternal reward awaits us, and nothing compares to this eternal reward. Paul intended all believers, including parents, to know "that from the Lord you will receive the reward of the inheritance. It is the Lord Christ whom you serve" (Colossians 3:24).

## "Well Done, Good and Faithful Servant!"

All Christian parents will one day stand before the Lord at the judgment seat of Christ (2 Corinthians 5:10; Romans 14:10). Our parenting will be part of this judgment. We will not be judged for our children's conduct toward us but for our conduct toward our children. We will hear His humble and true evaluation of our actions and reactions toward our kids. Hopefully, we will hear, "Well done," and receive the Lord's reward for our godly actions and reactions in the parenting process.

This is why it is so important that our parenting should be more unto the Lord than toward our kids. In the words of our Lord in Matthew 25, "Truly I say to you, to the extent that you did it to . . . even the least of them, you did it to Me" (v. 40). And as Paul put it in Ephesians 6:7–8: "Serve wholeheartedly, as if you were serving the Lord, not men, because you know that the Lord will reward everyone for whatever good he does" (NIV). Paul was saying that whatever we do as to the Lord we will receive back from Him, and that certainly includes parenting (which he addressed a few verses earlier in Ephesians 6:4). Everything you do as a mom or dad counts, even if your child ignores you. This is what the Family Rewarded Cycle is all about. God never ignores you!

Parents who feel discouraged can suddenly catch the truth that what they do matters to God; *nothing is wasted*. Putting on love toward a disrespectful child counts to God even if the child refuses to appreciate the love. These seemingly fruitless efforts matter to God because this is the kind of service He rewards. In other words, when our children refuse to respond to us but we still love them, the Lord rewards us as parents.

What are the rewards? We get some of them on earth, but we get an incredible reward in heaven. Jesus wants to say, "Well done, good and faithful servant! You have been faithful with a few things; I will put you in charge of many things. Come and share your master's happiness!" (Matthew 25:23 NIV). What would some of those "few things" be? Surely they include what Paul described as God's call to parents, which we studied under G-U-I-D-E-S. When you make a decision to parent God's way, the dividends are without end. Jesus is offering you a bargain. Do a few things on earth in this life and get many things forever in heaven.

Have you ever thought about what it will mean to "share your master's happiness"? It will be joy without measure. Think of your graduation day, wedding day, birthdays, children's birthdays, summer vacations, promotions, retirement, good times of all descriptions. What if every hour of every day you experienced the glory and joy of all these events at once in their fullest intensity? When you "share your master's happiness," the intensity will be trillions of times greater.

Envision the scene as believers ascend into heaven and stand before Christ. To a parent He says, "Well done. You've put on love toward your disrespectful child. I watched. You are about to be rewarded for every act of love."

As Christ-following parents we have the privilege of living with the end in mind, which is doing Christ's will and hearing His, "Well done, good and faithful servant." This is about pleasing Christ by the way we parent. In other words, parenting is a tool and test to deepen and demonstrate our love, reverence, trust, and obedience toward Jesus Christ.

But how do we stand the test? How does all this work in the daily battle? The next three chapters will deal with these questions. First, we need to ask His help to do the impossible—*unconditionally* love our kids.

# 13

# BECAUSE HE LOVES US, NO MATTER WHAT . . . WE LOVE THEM . . . NO MATTER WHAT

I t is not my husband and me who are on the Crazy Cycle, but it's me and our four kids! I know that when I react to them, then they react negatively toward me . . . there is a point where we love them as moms but don't like them. That is where I am at, and it drags us all down. We need help getting off the Family Crazy Cycle."

The mom who wrote this letter is not alone. Another mom commented, "One time while driving with my two toddlers and one preschooler crying in the car, *I* started to cry and said, 'What was I thinking?!' God spoke so clearly to me I almost had to pull over. He said, 'You weren't! I was!' That was freeing. Now when I tend to come to my wit's end, I say, 'Lord, this was *Your* idea. *Help!*'"

This mother of three little ones has the right approach. We all need help. When at the corner of Wit's End and Stress Avenue (which feels like a dead end), the follower of Christ can turn to the Helper—the Holy Spirit. In fact, God expects us to depend on

Him. If we don't, we will feel helpless and hopeless. Concerning growing our families, the psalmist warns against absolute self-reliance: "Without the help of the Lord it is useless to build a home" (Psalm 127:1 CEV).[1]

Another passage many families claim is Joshua 24:15: "As for me and my house, we will serve the Lord." When Sarah and I married, we made this verse part of our wedding ceremony. Our son Jonathan and his wife, also named Sarah, did as well. We have two plaques with Joshua 24:15 in our home. Joy has already claimed them as her own when we leave this earth.

Looking to the Lord for help . . . seeking to serve Him . . . of course . . . but how does that work in the heat of the daily battle, when the Family Crazy Cycle is dragging you under? One way to picture seeking His help, especially when your children are being irresponsible or even disrespectful, is to look just beyond their shoulders and see Jesus, ready to give you patience, strength, courage, perseverance—whatever you need

*Hear, O Lord, and be gracious to me; O Lord, be my helper.*

*—Psalm 30:10*

at the moment. Then utter a simple prayer, right to the point: "Help me, Jesus!"

The moment we cry to Him for help, He is already pleased. As He gives us strength to love our children, He smiles. By loving our children, we are showing our love to our Lord. We are parenting as unto Him.

When Christ declared, "Apart from Me you can do nothing" (John 15:5), He meant it. You cannot put on perfect love toward a disobedient, disrespectful, and defiant child—not every time. You wear no cape with an *S* on it. Your human nature cannot love perfectly. Add exhaustion to the mix, and the ingredients spell the Family Crazy Cycle at Mach 1: without love a child reacts without respect, and without respect a parent reacts without love. No one is happy.

The pressure only increases when we realize we are supposed to love our kids as He loves us—*unconditionally.* As I teach, counsel, and talk with wives and husbands, fathers and mothers, I often find "unconditional love or respect" a tough sell, especially among wives, who have been culturally conditioned to "respect their husbands only when they deserve it." But that is not what *unconditional* means, whether applying it to our spouses or our kids.

## The Real Meaning of *Unconditional*

By *unconditional* I mean that there is no condition that causes me to be unloving or disrespectful. In other words, if I am unloving or disrespectful, it is not because of certain circumstances caused by others that make me react unlovingly or disrespectfully. I *choose* to be harsh, independent of the circumstances.

As one parent admitted to me: "We tend to be Christlike when the kids are behaving and harsh when they are disobedient." Most of us can identify, but we know this is a long way from unconditional love; in fact it is the precise opposite. We cannot say, "I would unconditionally love my kids if they would just behave!" This is not about demanding that our kids be deserving of love and respect by being lovable and respectable. If we continue in this fashion, we will always love or respect our kids conditionally, depending on how they act. It is simple enough to make them scapegoats for our display of anger or impatience. But all this irresponsibility on our part lasts only so long. Eventually, the kids grow up, and the tables turn. As adults, our children can blame us for all their problems. Sadly, they make their case against us, as we did against them.

So where does that leave us with trying to love them unconditionally? To love unconditionally, we obey God's command to put on love or respect despite the circumstances (Romans 12:10; 1 Peter 2:17). If we refuse to obey this command, we end up rationalizing (telling ourselves "rational lies") and believing others have caused us to be harsh and rude. We tell others, in various ways, *they* made us react the way we did.

As parents we look to Jesus for motivation to love as He loves us—unconditionally. There is nothing we can do to get Him to loathe or despise us after we sin—nothing (Romans 8:1–2).

> *If you only love the lovable, do you expect a pat on the back? Run-of-the-mill sinners do that.*
>
> —*Luke 6:32 MSG*

However, though He loves us no matter what we do wrong, what we do wrong still matters to Him. This is why He disciplines us (Hebrews 12:5–11). In the same way, as parents, loving and respecting our kids unconditionally does not mean we remove all requirements and permissively give them license to do whatever.[2] We confront their failure to obey, and we discipline them by correcting their disrespectful attitude with a loving attitude. Unconditional love, then, means *we give our children the gift of a loving and respectful demeanor when they do not deserve it.* This is not about what they are failing to be; it is about what God is calling us to be.

From personal experience and from dealing with thousands of spouses and parents, I know loving unconditionally is impossible to do perfectly. I had to learn (more accurately, I am still learning) to love my children unconditionally; it does not come automatically. As I reflect on the years when our children were younger, I realize how often I did not even think of Jesus during a flare-up with the kids. There was a huge disconnect between my parenting and Christ. Instead of trying to imitate His unconditional love for me, I would be angry before I even thought of the Lord. Later, often with Sarah's urging, I would confess my sin to Him and apologize to my kids.

I would start again, and again, and again—trying to be more like Christ. I would try to remind myself that the Lord was present in my parenting and that He stood, so to speak, just beyond the shoulders of my children. I knew I had an audience of One to please and the kids were really secondary. I also knew the Lord was always willing to help me as I asked for His help with my irritation, presumption, preoccupation, sense of self-importance, anger, and defeats.

While I was turned off in great part by the poor example my own father set with his rage and loss of temper, nonetheless, his negative example came back to haunt me. I was seldom openly angry. Instead, it would boil within me as I felt my father's unwanted influence, which I had to counter. We all know the power of our "family of origin," as psychologists call it. Due to these issues, some of us struggle more in the parenting process than others. Yet we have the opportunity to receive help from the Holy Helper. Hear the testimony of Larry, a professor friend of mine and a man of great intellect, who discovered that family living is not a matter of right knowing but right doing:

> I know I cannot achieve this on my own and that this won't be easy. I have seen some aspects of my father rise up in me from time to time (when that happens, I stop and experience a "psychological vomit" because I am so repulsed). But relying on the Holy Spirit, I have experienced some of the fruits that God wants to come out of my life as detailed in Galatians 5:22–23.

Ultimately, I know that to break this cycle I must rely on God's resources and not my own. I can will myself to change, but this lasts only for a short period of time, then I fall back to my old habits. As a friend once told me, Galatians 5:22–23 describes the fruits of the Spirit, not the fruits of Larry.

And a mother wrote of her struggles:

I have been having immense struggles with obedience with my seven-year-old son. I have been burdened with a dislike for him as we engage in this Family Crazy Cycle. I don't want to be a part of it, but raising seven children ages thirteen to four months, with a husband that travels at times, I start to lose my purpose in serving the Lord. Your message today was so freeing . . . I was at my end, exhausted from my inability to break this cycle. I am going to look beyond him and see Christ. I am going to reflect on Scripture to show Jesus' love for him. I am going to let God do the work to mold him . . . I have been focusing on a few of his strengths and trying not to get wrapped up in a negative cycle of thoughts and anger . . . I keep my voice calm and focus on the correction to guide him. There have even been times when the Spirit has prompted me to just give him a big hug. I have seen some major changes within our relationship.

> Never pay back evil with more evil. Do things in such a way that everyone can see you are honorable.
>
> —Romans 12:17 NLT

A hurting father confessed:

In the heat of the moment, in the face of volatile defiance, everything goes out the window . . . I'm simply trying to survive the situation without saying anything that I will regret forever. My child has several variations of manipulative, defiant, disrespectful insolence toward us as parents, which causes us the desire to strike him. He is a really sweet kid with a kind and even overly sensitive heart, but who can, in a matter of fifteen minutes, infuriate us to the point where we just want to lock him in a room and run away from home. It can seem like Jekyll and Hyde . . . I no longer have much hope that when I meet the Lord I will hear, "Well done, good and faithful servant." I just hope He doesn't say, "I never knew you. Away from me, you evildoer."

We hear the pain and fear in this dad's words. Some of us can relate to his feelings of inadequacy. For this reason we need to come to grips with a straightforward truth: we cannot do G-U-I-D-E-S or any kind of positive, loving parenting on our own, and that's okay. When we feel disrespected, it is not natural to love or feel much love. However, it could be that God intends to use our kids to influence our lives more than He uses us to influence theirs. Parenting is not a one-way street. When that truth hit me, it changed the way I related to my kids.

## The Holy Spirit Is Called "Helper" for a Reason

Sarah and I found great encouragement from the fact that the Holy Spirit is called the Helper for a reason. God intends to help us because we need His help. It is okay—in fact, it is absolutely necessary—to admit that we are powerless to love perfectly a disrespectful and disobedient child. Many times in prayer Sarah and I expressed our powerlessness to parent His way. Instead of running from the feelings of inadequacy, we brought those feelings to the Lord. As the apostle Peter urged, we cast our anxiety on Him because we knew He cares for us (1 Peter 5:7).

Sarah and I did this kind of casting continually. In fact, Sarah says frequently, "I thought I was serious about growing spiritually until I had children. Then, after I had children, I really saw how much growing I had to do." In other words, children bring us to a point where we realize we do not have all the inner strength and wisdom in our spirit to be the kind of person we should be. At such moments, we can justify ourselves and blame our children, or we can acknowledge we need God. And along with this we need to realize that God is using our children in our lives, not just vice versa.

As we admitted our limitations and weaknesses, we discovered what Paul meant in 2 Corinthians 12:9: "My grace is sufficient for you, for my power is made perfect in weakness" (NIV). Sarah and I tried to apply this principle by bringing our weaknesses before Christ and asking for His gracious power to help us parent His way. We kept seeking to improve. Yet in our deepest hearts we recognized that we needed God first. We knew that God intended to use our children in our lives. Sarah gives testimony that she went deeper in faith and obedience as she learned how to give thanks in the face of things that she could not control. Sarah learned to praise and worship God during times of trial, and she had plenty of opportunities!

> *In certain ways we are weak, but the Spirit is here to help us.*
>
> —Romans 8:26 CEV

"Thanksgiving became my lifeline to the Lord," she says. "Giving thanks centers me on what God is able to do, keeps my prayers more positive, causes me to look to God for a solution rather than fixate on the problem, and brings a peace. Truly, I have peace in the waiting."

May I invite you and your spouse to acknowledge before the Lord that you, too, need His help? Perhaps you have been remiss in surrendering your family over to Christ more regularly. You have not prayed with any pattern, "Lord, not my will but Yours be done in this family." It is one thing to dedicate your children to the Lord in a service at church, an important event that many of us have done, but it is all too easy to forget to offer our kids to the Lord *continually*. Maybe you are trying too hard on your own. Perhaps the well-known expression, "Let God be God," applies especially to you right now. Memorize Zechariah 4:6, and pray it often as you go through your day with your children: "'Not by might nor by power, but by My Spirit,' says the LORD of hosts."

And here is a bonus: as we look to Christ for help, we can encourage our children to do the same. As we display our dependency on the Lord we can cultivate such faith in our kids. This is the way to build our homes. Already Jonathan and his wife have taught our two-year-old grandson, Jackson, Psalm 118:7: "Yes, the LORD is for me; he will help me" (NLT).

## What Unconditional Love Does *Not* Mean

If we are to love our kids unconditionally—regardless of their disobedience—it means we must come to grips with who we are as parents, independent of our children. As I mentioned, this family-of-origin stuff is very real for me. There were moments when I could feel it surging in me, just as I had seen it surge in my father. But I refused to let myself lose control. I slowed myself down, knowing my kids were just being kids even when appearing disrespectful. I knew the kids were not causing my sinful anger, any more than I caused my dad's sinful anger. That was my dad's issue, and if I had similar feelings, though far less intense and frequent, this was *my* issue.

Our kids do not cause us to sin but reveal our sinful choices. Unconditional love means there is no condition (circumstance or characteristic) that forces us to be harsh, even hateful, toward our children. Jesus taught: "For from within, out of the heart" come our sinful choices, which He lists in great number (Mark 7:21). Our children's disobedience or disrespect does not cause us to react in unloving ways. Our reaction comes from within.

The truth is, I choose harshness. My child does not choose harshness for me. But what about "firmness"? And where is the fine line between harsh and firm? Unconditional love does not mean I give my children license to disobey. I do not foolishly proclaim, "Go ahead and do whatever you want so that I can show you that I love you so much it makes no difference to me what you do." Unconditional love means that I lovingly confront their disrespectful and annoying behavior. I am loving even if they are rude and aggravating. Because they fail to be who they are supposed to be does not justify my failing to be who I'm supposed to be. I do not turn a blind eye to their wrongdoing, but I do not use their wrongdoing to justify being unloving.

Also, unconditional love does not equal unconditional trust. A mother loves her toddler no matter what, but she does not trust him to cross the street. The mother loves unconditionally, but she does not remove all conditions. Trusting the toddler to cross the street would be unloving.

Toward teens, we say, "I love you no matter what. Nothing you do, even lying, can ever make me stop loving you. My love is unconditional, *but* after you lie to me, I will not automatically trust you. If I trusted you blindly after you lied, I would not be very loving."

## Use G-U-I-D-E-S to Love Your Kids Unconditionally

In the last chapter we expanded the Family Rewarded Cycle to say that a parent's love is unto Jesus Christ and his child, regardless of the child's respect. In G-U-I-D-E-S we have a game plan to parent our children as unto Jesus. As we use these six strategies—actually they are responsibilities—they give us opportunity to imitate Jesus Christ apart from our children's responses.

G-U-I-D-E-S is all about how to love our children unconditionally. As the Lord loves us regardless of our behavior, we use G-U-I-D-E-S to love them regardless of their behavior. But how do we follow G-U-I-D-E-S while maintaining a proper balance between loving unconditionally and allowing for teachable consequences?

Here are some ideas:

Giving: we give to our kids because Christ is generous to us. We give (within reason) regardless of our child's gratefulness for our benevolence. When we withhold giving, we do so not because we are selfish but to prevent our child from being selfish.

Understanding: we understand our kids because Christ empathizes with us. We seek to understand our children regardless of their appreciation of our empathy. When we withhold sympathy, it is because we discern that our children are indulging in excessive self-pity. We care too much to celebrate their pity parties.

Instructing: we instruct our children because Christ imparts knowledge and wisdom to us. We instruct regardless of their receptivity. When we withhold information, we do so to allow them to learn through trial and error, not because we wish to sabotage their success.

**D**isciplining: we discipline our children because Christ confronts, corrects, and disciplines us. When necessary we enact consequences. When we withhold consequences, we do so as an act of mercy and grace, not because we fear the child's defiance and intimidation.

**E**ncouraging: we encourage our children to make a difference in their world because Christ calls us as adults to make a difference in our world. We cheer our children on even though they lack the social confidence and skill to defeat all foes. When we withhold affirming words, we do so to help them learn to stand strong on their own.

**S**upplicating: we supplicate for our kids because Christ intercedes for us. We pray for our children regardless of their spiritual interest or response. When we withhold prayer, we do so because it is time to step out in obedience, not to wait in faith.

G-U-I-D-E-S gives us the confidence to parent, knowing that what the kids do or do not do is secondary. This is about who we are, not about who our child fails to be. Regardless of our child's behavior, we will apply G-U-I-D-E-S. We will be who we have to be.

There is a story of an African boy who was captured by slave-runners and brought to America in the 1800s to be sold to the highest bidder. As he stood on the block to be auctioned off, a slave owner approached him and asked, "If I buy you, will you be honest?" The young man replied, "I will be honest whether or not you buy me."

As a loving parent I can say without hesitation, "I will be a giving person even though my child takes that for granted. I will be an understanding parent regardless of my child's warmth toward me. I will be an instructive parent even when my child listens to the wrong voices. I will discipline even though I am told that I am the worst parent on the planet. I will be an encouraging parent even though my child does not seem to receive my affirmation and comfort. And I will be a supplicating parent even though God seems silent and distant from me and my child."

G-U-I-D-E-S, in a nutshell, says: I have made a decision to be a loving parent, no matter what. Why? Because the Lord loves me no matter what. But there is still more to parenting God's way as unto Christ, and it involves not being ensnared in a very natural and human tendency. We will look at how to avoid this trap in the next chapter.

# 14

# BEWARE OF THE "OUTCOMES TRAP"

No matter how well we decode and defuse the Family Crazy Cycle and no matter how hard we work with G-U-I-D-E-S to make the Family Energizing Cycle hum, parenting is difficult, demanding, and for some, a defeating proposition. The truth is, we are not in control. Our kids are free moral agents. Ultimately, they will decide their inner attitudes and choices.

The Family Rewarded Cycle is there as our foundation—a mental picture if you will—to remind us of our identity in Christ and the rewards He has waiting. He is always there, just beyond our child's shoulder to help, and only He can give you the power to love your child unconditionally.

But the most important function of the Family Rewarded Cycle is to keep you from falling into the outcomes trap. I call it a trap because most of us are outcome based in our parenting, due in great part to being culturally conditioned to always want results. For example, in business we must get results, or the company can fold. In athletics, all coaches want results, from Little League to the pros. Anywhere you care to look, from dance lessons to piano lessons, from growing orchids to growing corn, we want results.

In just about any area we view the outcome as determining success or failure, and that includes parenting. When our children are "good" (they are obedient and make us proud), we see ourselves as successful, good parents. When our children are

> *Ultimately children choose to "obey their parents" (Colossians 3:20 CEV) or to be "disobedient to parents" (Romans 1:30; 2 Timothy 3:2).*

"bad" (they disobey, go against our values, embarrass or shame us), we see ourselves as failures, as bad parents.

The question we must settle in our minds is this: When we parent unto Christ, will our focus be on what God calls us to be, or will we shift our attention to trying to control the hearts and souls of our children?

## We Cannot Control the Final Outcome in Their Souls

I am convinced that to parent God's way with G-U-I-D-E-S as our game plan means that we do not consume ourselves with controlling the final outcome in our children. Ultimately the decisions of the soul (issues of faith and values) are up to each child. Our task is to focus on the process: to give, understand, instruct, discipline, encourage, and supplicate as we think best, while knowing that our children will ultimately decide on their own attitudes, beliefs, and actions.

Does this mean we become indifferent to the outcomes in our children? Absolutely not! We care about this more than our own lives. But the Bible is clear that children can go their own independent way as they move into adulthood. Ephesians 6:1 commands, "Children, obey your parents in the Lord, for this is right." God's command here is made to the children, not the parents. They are independent, moral, and spiritual beings who have the same freedom as their parents. They can obey God's commands or disobey.

God intended this limitation for all parents for the sake of the children. Yes, we must speak about these matters of the soul to our children and tell them what we desire, but we recognize this is their choice, not ours. And, yes, they must attend church with us (at least to a certain age), but ultimately they must choose if they will believe and attend church because they want to. A child's faith must become his own. Love must recognize free will.

In granting free will to children, God placed parents in a position to concentrate on what they are free to do: apply G-U-I-D-E-S. The good news is that when G-U-I-D-E-S is used humbly and patiently with children, it creates a loving environment that best influences them to choose their parents' faith and values. Positive modeling of our beliefs appeals far more to our children than barking commands to obey. Few things are more appealing to children than parents who are grateful, composed, teachable, obedient, courageous, and full of faith. We desire these inner virtues in our kids; do we see them in ourselves?

Sarah and I knew we needed God's help in modeling and our children needed His help in choosing, so we prayed for ourselves and for them. In fact, we believed that He allowed these limitations in us so that we would look to Him for help. Thus, we asked God to help us and our children each to . . .

- develop a thankful and grateful heart,
- have a calm and tranquil heart,
- have a teachable spirit,

- possess true remorse and a desire to change course for the good,
- have courage to do what God calls a person to do, and
- have a longing to trust and obey Him.

We daily spoke to God about God's speaking daily to our kids. We still pray this way though they are out of our home, living their lives independently of us.

## Do Good Parents Always Have Good Kids?

Family studies show there are two basic views on why children turn out as they do. The "Social Learning Theory" argues that children imitate their parents. They do as their parents did, good or bad. The "Compensatory Theory" contends that children counteract the parental example. They do not do as their parents did, good or bad.

Actually, both theories come into play in most families. It is not a clear case of either-or, but I constantly run into the idea that parents have almost absolute power to "predestine" their children to go one way or another, and the children are a clean slate with no say.

But what does the Bible say? Many Christian parents quickly point to Proverbs 22:6: "Train up a child in the way he should go, and when he is old he will not depart from it" (NKJV). Some parents think this is a promise from God that their children will follow Him. But this is a scriptural principle, not an absolute promise. Proverbs consists of pithy statements that are generally true but have exceptions. Look at Proverbs 26:4 versus 26:5. Answer a fool, but do not answer a fool! Or we read, "The reward of humility and the fear of the LORD are riches, honor and life" (Proverbs 22:4). Though this proverb is true, it is not always true. It is a principle, not a promise. There are many godly, humble people around the world who do not have riches. Does the lack of riches mean this poor person lacks humility and the fear of the Lord? Of course not! Proverbs reveals that there are exceptions to having riches. It is better to be poor, in order to maintain integrity (Proverbs 28:6, 11). Or what about proverbs that appear to promise long life for righteous living (3:2, 16; 4:10)? Did not Jesus die at age thirty-three, and have not many young believers died for their faith? Yes, a godly and wise life increases the likelihood of a long life, but persecution for one's faith can undercut longevity, which the Bible also reveals. Thus, in interpreting the Bible we must recognize every text of Scripture is to be interpreted in light of the larger context of Scripture. As for Proverbs, they reveal the better and best course but do not guarantee absolute outcomes since other conditions can come into play. With regard to the family, parents can train their children rightly according to Proverbs 22:6. Yet, Proverbs also teaches that kids can forsake a parent's teaching, and even despise, assault, rob, and curse them (Proverbs 1:8; 6:20; 19:26; 20:20; 23:22; 28:24; 30:11). In these texts the parents did not cause their kids to scorn, stab, steal, and swear.

Therefore, when considering Proverbs 22:6, we must recognize that some children depart from the faith. Ironically and sadly, Solomon wrote this proverb with his son Rehoboam in mind, and Rehoboam forsook the law of the Lord (2 Chronicles 12:1). Stunningly, Rehoboam grew up knowing that the Lord Himself had appeared to his dad two times (1 Kings 9:2) and that his father was the wisest man on the planet (1 Kings 4:30–31). The Bible does not offer a fail-safe formula to parenting.

Let's look at four different scenarios in the Bible that have been played out between parents and their children since Adam and Eve had Cain and Abel:

- Bad parents with bad children
- Bad parents with good children
- Good parents with good children
- Good parents with bad children

As we will see, both theories of parenting, Social Learning (the kids imitate their parents) and Compensatory (the children do not follow the parents), are illustrated in these different scenarios.

## Bad Parents with Bad Children

By bad parents I mean parents who refuse to trust and obey God and choose an evil lifestyle. They do not apply G-U-I-D-E-S. The children of these bad parents also refuse to trust and obey God.

One of many biblical examples is: "Ahaziah the son of Ahab became king over Israel in Samaria in the seventeenth year of Jehoshaphat king of Judah, and he reigned two years over Israel. He did evil in the sight of the LORD and walked in the way of his father and in the way of his mother and in the way of Jeroboam the son of Nebat, who caused Israel to sin" (1 Kings 22:51–52). Ahaziah chose to follow in the footsteps of his father, Ahab, and his mother, Jezebel. Some children do "as their fathers did" (2 Kings 17:41).

I think of Herodias, who counseled her daughter to ask for the head of John the Baptist and her daughter obliged her. "Having been prompted by her mother, she said, 'Give me here on a platter the head of John the Baptist'" (Matthew 14:8).

We all recognize the enticement that comes to children to go the way of evil when parents live sensual lives. Isaiah describes such a scene. "But come here, you sons of a sorceress, offspring of an adulterer and a prostitute. Against whom do you jest? Against whom do you open wide your mouth and stick out your tongue? Are you not children of rebellion, offspring of deceit?" (Isaiah 57:3–4).

Down through the centuries the bad-to-bad scenario has continued. Some parents subject their children to abuse and violence. These kids are exposed to horrific cruelty. But eventually these victimized children choose whether or not they will victimize others. Will the bullied child in the home become the bully outside the home? The bullied child ultimately decides this. He is not predestined for bullyhood, and this is the good news about free will.

Children always have a future choice, even if in the past their parents dragged them into drugs or subjected them to physical or sexual abuse. I maintain this, not to excuse the parent's evil (which will be judged by our Lord) or to minimize the tough obstacles these children will have to overcome, but to assert that they are not doomed to a life of doing bad.

The proof of free will and the power of choice is in the next scenario.

### Bad Parents with Good Children

There are parents who have chosen evil, yet their children choose to trust and obey God. How so? Kids are moral and spiritual beings who can choose God's path regardless of their parents.[1] Though this is not easy for a child, the good news here is that children are not hopeless and helpless victims. I would never say to a child, "You are fated to do the bad that was done to you." That is true cruelty.

As a young boy I took the compensatory route and almost always tried to counteract my dad's negative influence. Few things can hurt a young boy as much as what my father did: in one of his rages he tried to strangle my mother, and later he committed adultery. But something told me I had the freedom to choose a different direction from my dad, and I did. I compensated, dealing with struggles my classmates did not know. I believe I had greater insight and incentive to travel a different road because I saw firsthand how I did not want to live.

My father and I are reflected in Ezekiel 18, which tells of one man who does evil and faces judgment,[2] but his son "sees all the sins his father commits, and though he sees them, he does not do such things" (v. 14 NIV).

In another case from Scripture we see Manasseh, one of the most evil of Judah's kings, having a son, Amon, who followed in his footsteps (bad dad, bad son). But King Amon's son, Josiah, became king at age eight, and "he did what was right in the eyes of the LORD" (2 Chronicles 34:2 NIV). Despite a grandfather and father who did not obey God, Josiah reigned for over three decades and brought about great reforms in Judah. He pleased God, and when he found the Book of the Law in the eighteenth year of his reign, even greater things transpired (2 Chronicles 34:3–33).

My files are full of testimonies from children who decided not to go the way of parents who were not interested in pleasing the Lord. One man wrote: "My father and his father were both screamers and yellers. I resolved long ago that I would never be that way."

Bad parents do not control how the game will end. Even children who may not know the Lord are still able to make good choices despite a parent's bad example, but the obstacles can be great. Bad parenting can cause all sorts of long-term misery for children, apart from the healing power of God's grace.

So I am not excusing mistakes we make as parents, nor am I saying that God gives poor parenting a pass. Bad parents will be judged and good parents rewarded. We will all give an account to God on our parenting. Jesus said, "Whoever causes one of these little ones who believe in Me to stumble, it would be better for him to have a heavy millstone hung around his neck, and to be drowned in the depth of the sea" (Matthew 18:6).

These are heavy words of warning. Jesus' word choice of "stumble" is significant. The Greek word used here is *skandalon*, from which we get "scandal." Used in Greek it can have several meanings, including a trigger in a trap, a snare, or an impediment placed in another's way. And the word is also used regarding a "cause of offense" or "causing another to sin." Jesus' use of it here could even be interpreted to imply a parent sticking out a foot, causing the child to stumble. In Jesus' eyes, woe to the parent who tricks, entices, or causes a child to fall into sin. Drowning is too good for him.

But the good news is that the word *stumble* suggests the child's ability to get back up and choose good rather than evil. Thus, even with cruel parenting, free will exists for the child.

But what of the scenarios where the parents are "good"? I assume most of you reading this book fall into this category, or you would not be reading a book on how to parent God's way.

First, the ideal situation . . .

## Good Parents with Good Children

This is what every Christian family hopes and prays will happen. Mom and dad believe and trust in God and try to practice good parenting such as the principles in G-U-I-D-E-S. Again, we find examples of this in Scripture. In Luke we meet the priest Zacharias and his wife, Elizabeth, who were both "righteous in the sight of God, walking blamelessly in all the commandments" (Luke 1:6). Although Elizabeth was barren, God chose to give her a son, John the Baptist (Luke 1:7–25, 57–80). John was the forerunner of Jesus, who said of him, "Among those born of women there has not arisen anyone greater than John the Baptist!" (Matthew 11:11).

Another New Testament example is Paul's protégé Timothy, whose mother, Eunice, and grandmother Lois raised him to trust God (2 Timothy 1:5; 3:14–15).

The wonderful truth about good parents with good kids versus bad parents with good kids is that the good parents typically make it easier for their children to choose the good since they paint a picture of what it looks like with their own lives. But in either case the children ultimately make this good choice for themselves.

While we rejoice with godly parents whose children also choose God's way, I would like to warn these parents of a few pitfalls.

I often hear from good parents who have good kids, but these parents are still unhappy. One man of God in my congregation opened up to me about his son, saying, "Oh, my heart breaks over him." I asked, "Why?" This dad answered, "He is not having consistent devotions." I then asked, "Does he honor you?" "Oh yes," he replied. "Does he know Christ?" "Oh yes, he knows the Lord."

My friend had a standard, and because his son was not living up to that standard completely, he was disappointed with his parenting and his son. Perfectionism can be a heavy burden, especially for good parents who have good kids but who still are not perfect. Are you guilty of fixating on your children's mistakes and overlooking many good things? Be careful that you do not cause your good kids to lose heart.

Another pitfall for the perfectionistic parent, or even the *good* parent, is coming off as self-righteous. If, by the grace of God, your children are all serving the Lord and not challenging your spiritual guidance, it is all too easy to assume the outcome is due to your good parenting. But remember that Scripture does not support this assumption. Furthermore, patting yourself on the back can be premature and can also alienate your brothers and sisters in the Lord who are struggling with less compliant children. Even comments such as the following can heap guilt upon other good parents: "That girl turned out well because she had super parents who homeschooled her and sheltered her from temptations that kids her age faced." Or "He is in the ministry today because his father and grandfather were preachers. He comes from a great family."

Or how about what this person wrote to me: The good parent is "the exception and not the rule. I truly believe it does start at home and have found when kids go astray, the underlying root is usually at the heart of the home, when there is an absence of some moral fiber."

There is an element of truth in each of these statements, but what about the children who rebelled despite having parents who homeschooled and sheltered them from temptations? Or the family of generations of preachers whose offspring not only didn't go into the ministry but also walked away from the faith?

We cannot have it both ways. If we subscribe to the notion that children of good parents are destined for sainthood, then we must also believe that children of bad parents have no hope of a better life. But it is demoralizing to the children of bad parents if they have no freedom to compensate and pursue a better direction, but can only imitate the bad. These children might claim, "God is unfair!" It is also demoralizing to good parents when their children rebel against the faith, since their kids were supposed to imitate their holiness, not counteract the things of God. These parents might claim, "God is unfair!" Many parents end up in a crisis of faith basing their theology on these half-truths that are not supported by Scripture.

> *When they measure themselves by themselves and compare themselves with themselves, they are without understanding.*
>
> —2 Corinthians 10:12

Perhaps you identify with this mom, who was bold enough to say what many of us feel like saying from time to time:

> The Christian community is into comparison. There is an expectation to have perfect children who obey you and love Jesus. If they don't, it is a failure on your part. You are a poor role model and poor parent. For myself I feel judged by parents who have the kids who *love* church and are passionate about Jesus. My kids don't love church. I feel worse because I have been in ministry for a long time, and my kids aren't like "other ministry kids." I have an internal condemnation inner script that I am fighting.

## Good Parents with Bad Children

It's to this final group that I want to give special encouragement. My files are full of examples of good parents having kids who went "bad," or at least made very wrong choices at odds with the heart of Christ. Here are just a few:

- A friend of mine, a committed Christian, was and still is a great dad. But his two adult children both divorced their spouses, causing many family problems that almost swamped him and his wife emotionally.

- Another family I know had two children who walked away from the faith though both parents lived godly, humble lives. They loved their kids deeply, but their kids still rejected their faith.

- An adult son wrote to tell me of how his addiction to pornography turned his marriage upside down, almost ending in divorce. Yet, he had grown up in a great home with godly parents who were influential Christian leaders.

- And countless stories come to me about families with several children where one walks away from the church and gets addicted to alcohol or some other drug, while his siblings join Bible studies, pray with their parents, and love Jesus.

I hear every one of these parents loud and clear, and I share bits and pieces of their stories to make one point—perhaps the most important point in this entire book. They vividly illustrate the choice we all have as we parent our kids from the cradle to adulthood: Will I focus on the *outcomes*, constantly hanging on the cliff of "How did it go? How well did my child perform?" Or will I focus on the game plan and the *process*, doing as well as I can to parent God's way and trusting Him with the final result? This is no minor decision, nor can we make it only once. It comes up again and again.

But the burden good parents carry when their children are rebellious is a heavy one. We all know families where this happens. It may be happening in yours, and it is to you I want to give special encouragement. Some in the church fear that if we say parents are not absolutely responsible for their bad children, we are letting these parents off the hook. But are parents of "bad" children necessarily bad? When we guilt-trip innocent parents, we cause some of them to feel betrayed by God, in that He did not do what they felt He "promised" (Proverbs 22:6) to do in their kids since they were good parents.

Again, let's see what the Bible says.

A profound example of a good parent whose kids turned out badly is the prophet Samuel. Scripture tells us that when he was old Samuel appointed his sons, Joel and Abijah, judges over Israel. Samuel must have had some kind of idea his grown sons would do well in this important position, but alas, Samuel's sons "did not walk in his ways, but turned aside after dishonest gain and took bribes and perverted justice" (1 Samuel 8:3).[3]

In light of Samuel's godly upbringing, and faithful life of ministry in calling the Israelites to repent and follow God, it seems dumbfounding that his two sons chose such fraudulent ways. But when we remember that *all* are born sinners with free choice, it is not so dumbfounding after all. As the prophet Micah exclaimed: "For son treats father contemptuously, daughter rises up against her mother, . . . a man's enemies are the men of his own household" (Micah 7:6).

Consider also the story of the prodigal son (Luke 15:11–32). Most Christian parents know the parable well. Both of the sons in the story are what we might call misfits. The younger boy illustrates the extreme of unrighteous debauchery; the older son is a prime example of selfrighteousness and lack of forgiveness. What church would ask this dad to teach them how to parent God's way? Yet, Jesus used this father to demonstrate the character of God the Father, our model. No matter how this father felt at any point in the story, Jesus did not say one bad thing about him. All parents who are trying their best to love God and their children need to study this parable to see what God values in parents. If your children are not perfect, if your children are definitely rebelling, you need not shame yourself relentlessly, but instead work on maintaining a loving environment—an environment that might allow a rebellious child to return home without fear of shame and rejection.

When we feel crippling discouragement by the sinful choices and outcomes in our kids, we must not let this permanently deter us from parenting God's way: applying G-U-I-D-E-S as unto Him. I have seen many such families years later, and these same rebellious children are serving Christ in wonderful ways. God is always at work!

Stay the course regardless of the child's respect and obedience. This is the Family Rewarded Cycle: a parent's love unto Christ regardless of the child. You cannot control the outcome, but there is something you can control completely. We will look at that in the next chapter.

# 15

# My Response Is My Responsibility

It is one thing to understand we must avoid the outcomes trap. We can agree that we are not in control of the ultimate outcome with our children. So the question becomes:

What *can* I control?

The obvious answer is me, specifically my actions and reactions with my kids. In our Love & Respect conferences, Sarah makes a point that is as profound as it is simple, when she asks the audience, "Why should we expect our children to obey us when we are not obeying God?"

This challenging question is in direct contrast to the hypocrisy in the well-known phrase, "Do as I say, not as I do." If we want God to honor our efforts to parent with G-U-I-D-E-S, "doing what seems best" (Hebrews 12:10), then we must honor Him. Only then can we trust that "what seems best" will be the best we can do at any given moment because we trust Him for wisdom and direction.

All three cycles of parenting with Love & Respect bid us to ask another basic question as we move through our typical parenting duties on any given day:

Who is responsible for what is going on?

When I get on the Family Crazy Cycle, will I blame my child for wrongly feeling unloved and for reacting with disrespect? Or will I focus on my part of the craziness and start reacting in more loving ways? Will I give all the power over to my child or will I believe that God has put me in a position to be able to exercise the greater influence?

*Every parent must hear the Lord's question: "Why do you . . . honor your sons above Me . . . ?" And it is here the famous biblical saying comes into play, and it is about parenting: "for those who honor Me I will honor" (1 Samuel 2:29, 30).*

When it comes to the Family Energizing Cycle, will I demand that my child be respectful in order to motivate me to love, or will I expect myself to be more loving in order to influence my child's respect?

When it comes to the Family Rewarded Cycle, will I explode in anger if my child does not show me respect as to the Lord, or will I focus on showing love toward my child as to the Lord?

We may be able to force or convince our kids to conform to our rules, but only they will decide their own inner attitudes. Realistically then, we will focus on controlling our own attitudes, actions, or reactions. This is not to say that we parent passively. We still must take charge. A parent who is not in charge is not parenting, but simply trying to survive.

For example, as we instruct and discipline, we expect obedience. We teach our child to say, "Thank you," when given a gift or some other favor; at the same time, we know the limitations. We can only urge gratefulness, not coerce it. If the child refuses to say, "Thank you," we can assign logical discipline, but we cannot say, "You *will* be grateful; I demand it!" We can only set an example of being grateful and pray the child develops genuine feelings of gratitude.

When I speak of "being in charge," the first person I must be in charge of is . . . me. My response is my responsibility. As we create a loving environment and take responsibility for our responses and reactions, it increases our credibility. Our children are always watching us, and they can spot hypocrisy at a very young age. If we want our children to make heartfelt choices that are in keeping with what we are trying to teach them, the best possible combination is to be loving and in charge at the same time, modeling the behavior we desire for them to emulate. For instance, if we yell at our children to stop yelling, it simply means we have lost emotional control, and our children know it. You can be right but wrong at the top of your voice!

*Young mothers are to "be self-controlled" (Titus 2:4–5 NIV). Their response is their responsibility.*

Keeping emotional control while staying in charge means maintaining a delicate balance between forcing compliance and winning it. You may stop a child's disrespectful comments or behavior with harsh words or actions, but you will lose his heart and any chance for real and credible influence. My father got me to comply at some levels with his angry huffing and puffing, but deep inside I shut down on him. He lost my heart, and my mother could see it. This was a big reason why she arranged for me to leave home as a young teenager and attend military school, over two hundred miles away.

*Presumably married with a family, "young men" are to "be self-controlled" (Titus 2:6 NIV). Their response is their responsibility.*

# My Response—Good or Bad—
# Is My Responsibility

The phrase "My response is my responsibility" has an intriguing ring. When I use it at a conference, people nod in agreement and listen up. But what exactly do I mean? I explain by pointing out that my child does not *cause* me to be the way I am but rather *reveals* the way I am. Therefore when my response is sinful, I must own up to this as my issue. I must not blame my negative response on my child. I must live with it and try to change. And, if I have a loving response, doing my best to parent God's way, and my child is still being disrespectful, I must live with that and pray for patience. Bottom line, my response *is* my responsibility.

Parents often tell me, "But my child makes me react and respond in unloving ways . . . he can be a monster!" I understand; I really do. But an unlovable or disrespectful child does not make or cause us to be unloving. Instead, the child *reveals our choice to be unloving.*

By way of analogy, a speck of sand in the human eye leads to irritation, then infection, and if not cared for, loss of vision. That same speck of sand in an oyster first leads to irritation, then concretion, and then a pearl. This begs the question: Did the sand cause the results in the eye or the oyster? No. The sand is an irritant that reveals the inner properties of the human eye or the oyster. If that is not the case, the next time you get sand in your eye, be careful; a pearl may pop out.

Our kids can be irritants, and they reveal our inner properties as a person and parent.

Does that mean children are completely innocent in setting the tone for the family? Of course not. Children are moral and spiritual beings who make their own choices and affect us emotionally, but that does not mean their bad behavior *causes* our bad behavior. Being a good parent is our *choice*. Having a good parent-child relationship is a cooperative effort, and not all children cooperate. That is where G-U-I-D-E-S can come to our rescue.

## G-U-I-D-E-S—Best Way to "Parent as Unto Christ"

When we react in sinful and immature ways, we not only render ourselves less effective in impacting the outcomes in our kids; we end up disobeying God's commands to us and then experience guilt, defeat, and discouragement. On the other hand, when we focus on applying G-U-I-D-E-S, we are more consistent. We have a game plan and remain more cool, calm, and collected. Parenting as unto Christ regardless of a child's response becomes a gratifying, empowering process.

We are like the parent in a parable Jesus told about a man who had two sons: "He went to the first and said, 'Son, go and work today in the vineyard.' 'I will not,' he answered, but later he changed his mind and went. Then the father went to the other son and said the same thing. He answered, 'I will, sir,' but he did not go. Which of the two did what the father wanted? 'The first,' they answered" (Matthew 21:28–31 NIV).

Jesus went on to make a profound point about who would get into the kingdom, but I see a secondary application here for parents. One son said no but later obeyed. The other son said yes but later disobeyed. My son Jonathan was like the first son. He would argue with me or disagree because he did not want to do anything behind my back. Other children are like the second son: they will go along with their parents while in their presence, but later we discover they did not do as we asked. This kind of child is good at creating alibis and smiling in a way that gets us to be more lenient than we should at his disobedience.

Bottom line: if you have a defiant child, do not be so quick to conclude you are a failure; if you have a compliant child, do not think you are a total, lasting success.

Parents must postpone absolute judgments on their parenting effectiveness. A defiant fourteen-year-old may turn compliant at eighteen. A compliant eight-year-old can turn defiant at sixteen. Yes, we must deal with the defiance. Parenting does not cease. However, we always do what we know for sure: apply G-U-I-D-E-S. Give appropriately. Understand empathetically. Instruct clearly. Discipline fairly. Encourage positively. And supplicate faithfully.

If we apply G-U-I-D-E-S "as seems best" every day, over time our children will respond more respectfully. Our kids are much more likely to see us as "the real deal." This kind of modeling motivates. Such authenticity wins the day if anything will.

## What About Dealing with My Anger?

Does using G-U-I-D-E-S mean we should never get angry? When we talk about controlling our actions and reactions, does that mean we only have positive reactions and no negative reactions? The Bible describes an abundance of words that capture amoral, involuntary emotions—such feelings as anguish, grief, sadness, woe, despair, and misery. (And need I say kids bring us incredible joy?) Involuntary emotions do not constitute sin. Read the Psalms. As parents, for example, we will be sad and angry over our child's stealing, lying, or cheating. This is normal. To be a loving parent does not mean you must be a robot.

Many believers are familiar with Ephesians 4:26: "Be angry, and yet do not sin." In other words, there is a place for righteous parental indignation. When a sixteen-year-old lies to his teacher about not getting his homework done because of "sickness" and forges the parent's signature vouching for his lie, a parent ought to get angry. A parent can say, "I am extremely angry over what you have chosen to do. I need time to cool down, and when I do, you will receive the consequences of your unwise decision."

> Parents are not androids. They feel the full range of emotions. "A wise son brings joy to his father, but a foolish son brings grief to his mother" (Proverbs 10:1 NIV).

With amoral or involuntary emotions, parents must strive not to step over the moral line. That is why Scripture tells us, "Be angry, and yet do not sin." In getting angry, a parent can get too angry. Note that Ephesians 4:26 goes on to say, "Do not let the sun go down on your wrath" (NKJV). The point is, do not let angry feelings stay and fester.

Self-control does not mean we refrain from giving voice to strong feelings. We express what we are feeling, but we control that expression. We need to state these feelings in such a way that we have no regret about how we communicated.

How do we know when we step over the line into a sinful reaction? Typically, the conscience speaks clearly enough about where that line is. If unsure, seeking counsel from godly, wise people can help us clarify this. Also, our kids can certainly tell us as we see their crushed spirit and fear.

A mother responded to my teaching about anger by writing:

There is no way I cannot get angry, sad, and more at this child. However, this makes me know that the initial feelings are okay . . . it is what I do with those feelings that really matters before God and my child. I do love the thought that God does see and will reward when I love this unlovable and sometimes disrespectful child. That gives me hope because she certainly doesn't appreciate it when I do.

Perhaps you identify with this mother. She must hang in there. So must we all. Parenting—especially controlling one's feelings—is a marathon, not a sprint.

## What About Anger and the Devil?

Note that after Paul tells us to be angry but not to sin, he says: "Do not give the devil a foothold" (Ephesians 4:27 NIV). Do you ever get so upset that you say and do things that simply are not you? Do you comment afterward, "I don't know what came over me. I just wasn't myself. I have no idea what possessed me"? These are the times that comedian Flip Wilson was referring to when he said, "The devil made me do it!" Paul says in verse 26 not to let the sun go down on our wrath. Why? Because the devil can take advantage of our prolonged anger.

Satan deceives us by intensifying our angry emotions to the point that we suddenly are no longer ourselves. Though he does not possess us, he does oppress us. At such moments in the family, we resist him by being slow to anger (James 1:19) and by ending that anger before sunset (Ephesians 4:26). If not, he takes a foothold and schemes against us by tricking us into more emotional craziness. (Note that Ephesians 6:11, 16 follows 6:4.) We must not take lightly the idea of the devil, as though he is an imaginary character in red tights with a pitchfork. The Bible declares that he "prowls around like a roaring lion, seeking someone to devour" (1 Peter 5:8).

Every parent must recognize the seriousness of this teaching. When I was eighteen and had been a Christian for two years, I was home for the summer, before my first year of college, when my father displayed one of his fits of rage about something. Instead of my usual avoidance, I turned to him and said, "Who has control of you right now? Is it the devil?"

My dad immediately went limp and said, "Yes, I think so."

I did not say it disrespectfully. I said it out of a concern for what I was observing in him. It appeared demonic. I had seen this countless times before but had never made this comment. In this instance I felt as though I was a young adult talking to another adult. Thankfully, he received my question and ceased his raging, which shocked me. He quieted down and walked off. Within months my dad came to Christ.

I realize that behind closed doors many families encounter this kind of thing. We must not look around for someone to point at; we must look within ourselves. If anything like this is taking place within your soul, you need to realize that this is a crucial moment to make a serious adjustment. Your children are not making you angry. You are choosing to be angry and the enemy of your soul seeks to "amp up" your lingering anger. This is not just a parenting matter; it is your spiritual battle. This is about your anger and the powers of darkness (Ephesians 6:10–12).

I rejoice in getting letters such as this one, from a mother who was aware of the danger in rage and was calling on the Lord:

I had no idea what I would be dealing with when my seventeen-year-old son picked us up at the airport Saturday night after the Love and Respect seminar. I was heavily convicted of how disrespectful I had been over the years to . . . my children. I have two sons, nineteen and seventeen . . . My husband and I are healing rage-aholics, and suffice it to say, my children are a product of this battleground. When I got in my son's car, I saw that he had not cleaned his car as I had demanded when he drove me to the airport. . . . Well, I went ballistic. My husband was in the front seat with my son and asked me to please stop, in a very loving, quiet way. I mocked him under my breath, but loud enough that they could both hear me above the radio, and continued my tirade off and on.

She goes on to say that after they arrived home, the house was not clean, and this led to a more heated argument. Her husband kindly asked her to leave the room. She continued:

The seminar had been my idea, and now what in the world was I doing? I did leave the room, and practically crawled to my bedroom in shame and pain . . . I said, "Lord, I am unrighteous and unholy, and I don't want to act like this anymore . . . I can't do it, I can't be respectful to my husband and my sons." But God is righteous and holy, and He can do it for me if I do it unto Him . . . I was left alone with my son who still refused to clean up the house . . . He became angry and was throwing things . . . I looked my son in the eyes and said to myself, "Lord, how am I going to respect my son and still stick to my guns without being afraid of him, crying, or getting angry?" An amazing peace came over me and a resolve I have never felt before. My son raged, it felt like ten minutes, still throwing things . . . I persisted, quietly, respectfully, calmly, telling him that he needed to clean up all the mess . . . He did clean it all up . . . God did a wonderful thing today, He showed me hope in the face of adversity . . . While I was writing this, my nineteen-year-old son called from college just to tell me he loves me!! He n-e-v-e-r does that, so God is giving me a tasty morsel of love!

## Controlling Anger Does Not Mean Compromising

We see above that when parents fixate on their children's misbehavior (the outcome) and do not focus on their own actions, they will forget their G-U-I-D-E-S game plan and slip into angry reactions. But in warning against uncontrolled anger I am not endorsing parental passivity or indulgence.

I learned of one adult son who said the thing that disappointed him the most about his parents is that they compromised their spiritual convictions. Because he was rebelling in his teens, they gave in and compromised. To have some peace they let him do something they all knew was wrong. He looks back with great pain and disappointment over this. Not only did guilt overcome him because he felt he caused his parents to compromise their convictions, but their concession caused him to question if they truly believed. Their compromise undermined his faith. He thought, *If Mom and Dad did not stand strong, then perhaps these are not convictions worth living for. Perhaps what they told me is untrue.* In "kicking the fencepost," he had subconsciously hoped it would be sturdy. Instead, it gave way.

Sometimes a parent can compromise, if it is something that

is a question of taste or opinion, but when something is clearly a violation of biblical truth, being passive and "reasonable" only compromises Christ.

When I address the importance of parents controlling their actions and reactions, please understand that I am not trying to squeeze all of us into a mold of perfectionism. We might start the day with perfection in mind, but getting three kids ready for school can be like herding stray cats. Then putting three kids in the backseat of a car is like putting three cats in a potato sack; the screeching and shrieking can be deafening. No parent controls the kids and remains perfectly cool, calm, and collected 24/7. Kid stuff happens!

So let's agree. We all would be perfect parents if it were not for our children. Fortunately, God's mercy and grace are always there on the heels of our failings. To paraphrase Proverbs 24:16: "A righteous parent falls seven times, and rises again." Get back up. Don't quit. Rebound. Start again. Give yourself some slack and keep using G-U-I-D-E-S to parent God's way. Over the long haul, we cannot control the outcome; that is up to our kids and God's sovereign will. But we can control our actions and create important moments between us and our children—the kind of moments that build a lasting positive legacy. We are all building some kind of legacy. We will look at what that can mean as we conclude this book on parenting with love and respect in your family.

# Conclusion

# What Kind of Legacy Will You Leave?

Legacy. What do we want to leave our children? A fitting question for concluding this book.

For certain, we long for our children to remember and feel that we loved them, and I believe that when we apply the principles set forth in this book, most of us will have kids testifying at our caskets, "My parents loved me and loved me well."

From our caskets?

Yes.

One of the best principles to live by is "Begin with the end in mind." Beyond business practices, this has life application. Knowing we will die, we work back from our death. This gives us perspective for today. Death should never be morbid but motivating. In fact, we derive wisdom when asking, "How am I living today in light of my death?" Somewhere in the back of our brains this question needs to hover. We need to keep an active file entitled "Funeral Day." Knowing that our lives come to an end should guide our parenting.

I receive e-mails from people who remind me to keep the end in mind. I am always stirred. A friend and husband wrote:

> It was on this day one year ago that Diane, my dear wife of twenty-eight years and mother of my daughters, was taken to heaven, leaving earth with a strong sense of dignity and grace after dealing with a long bout of cancer . . . While we miss Diane's physical presence, we have realized this past year what a strong legacy of love she leaves with us . . . I believe this is a tribute to Diane and how well she prepared us, and the legacy of her love for us that remains.

A wife wrote to me about her deceased husband:

> The Lord got hold of his heart. He was a changed man after that. Yes, we still had some bridges to cross but we crossed them together. We had such a beautiful marriage. We grew closer each day and the Lord worked in both our lives. We were implementing Love and Respect . . . The Lord called my dear husband home almost sixteen months ago after a short illness. I was sitting by his side when he took his last breath and stepped into the arms of his waiting Lord. He left our children (we have five children), our grandchildren, our great-grandchildren, and me a wonderful legacy. I do not know and have never known anyone who loved the Lord more than my husband did.

These, indeed, are stories of a legacy.

Sadly, some of us major on the minors and sweat the small stuff. The urgent replaces the important. We are too anxious and fixed on temporary things that in the end do not matter, and in the end what does matter, we overlook. Some of us are wired way too tight about minutiae. I tell folks at our conferences, "Lighten up. You're going to die." Bellowing laughter arises from the audience. People get the point because it is too often true. But few of us want to waste our parenting privilege. Who wants to be ashamed at the end about how we raised our kids and lived our lives? Who desires to be a soul who reacted to the trivial and ignored the timeless?

A father wrote me from Australia after reading what I said about leaving a legacy, "Then, 'Bam!' I got to the sentence near the end of the book about the negative legacy you leave your kids if you keep getting it wrong! It was like I could feel a missile go right through me." He determined to get it right.

This idea of legacy weighs heavily with most of us. A couple wrote: "We enjoyed the journey of moving from Crazy Cycle to motivated and Energized Cycle and now believing God on the Rewarded Cycle to become part of our relationship. We are eternally grateful as we leave a legacy for our kids and grandkids."

This is the legacy we leave with our kids, based on G-U-I-D-E-S:

- They will feel cared for because we lovingly gave.
- They will feel empathized with because we lovingly understood.
- They will feel equipped because we lovingly instructed.
- They will feel self-controlled because we lovingly disciplined.
- They will feel courageous because we lovingly encouraged.
- They will feel divinely guided because we lovingly supplicated.

## Living Examples of a Powerful Legacy

An adult son wrote about his father, recalling that he went bankrupt one year short of retirement. He was a partner in a large brokerage firm. He lost everything and entered retirement almost penniless. Unsuccessful cataract surgery followed, and he went partially blind. He developed angina and later, Alzheimer's, passing away at seventy-seven. Through all the setbacks his father's faith "never faltered." Although he endured sufferings akin to Job, any doubts about God's love for him never even crossed his mind. The son said in closing: "How did all of this affect me? Let me put it this way: with this kind of example, it's pretty hard to rationalize doing bad things when times get tough."

This is called a legacy left in the soul of a child.

*This is not about your kids but about you! Remember, "When he comes, he will bring out in the open and place in evidence all kinds of things we never even dreamed of—inner motives and purposes and prayers. Only then will any one of us get to hear the 'Well done!' of God"* (1 Corinthians 4:5 MSG).

I know of a man who has four sons. As they grew up, they would sit at the dinner table after church and listen to their dad share about how God spoke to his heart. They saw a dad, who himself had a dad who committed suicide and left an incredible wound inside, but he allowed God to heal him. They saw a dad wanting to trust God more. They saw a dad desiring to learn what the Bible had to say on life issues. They saw a dad stand around with other men and talk about Christ. They saw a man pray at the table from his heart. They observed a man get really angry at them but then come back later with head bowed and seek forgiveness. They saw a man be content with his salary. They saw a man who was there for them. They saw a man who loved his wife. They observed a man with a prayer list. They saw a man who wanted to be used of God in the lives of other people. They saw a man who was teachable. Guess who loves God besides dad?

This is called a legacy left in the soul of one's children.

Is there anything greater?

Actually, we must say there is something different, maybe not better. Not all children will inherit our legacy. They will take a different path. So where does that leave us?

Sarah tells audiences at our Love & Respect conferences, "This is all about me." When she makes this statement everyone has a puzzled look: *Did she say what I just thought she said? Did she say we need to be narcissistic?*

Sarah continues, "Yes, this truly is all about me. At the Judgment the Lord will ask me, 'Did you trust and obey Me? Did you love and reverence Me in your marriage and family?'"

She then makes it clear, "This is all about my following the Lord, no matter the responses of others."

Sarah and I have prayed one prayer more than any other prayer: "So teach us to number our days, that we may present to You a heart of wisdom" (Psalm 90:12). I know when I have prayed this, I have envisioned the end of my days, standing before the Lord. In my heart I wonder, *Will I present to Him a heart that was wise to the end? Will I finish faithful? Will I have done what God called me to do as a parent and person?* As much as I hurt over the thought of my children not asking these questions, and nothing pains me more, I realize that at the end this is between Jesus and me.

Hopefully I will hear:

- "You loved your children well, doing so out of trust and obedience toward Me, and from a love and reverence for Me even though they walked a different path."
- "You kept on giving from a generous heart even when your children were ungrateful."
- "You continually tried to understand from an empathetic heart even when your children claimed that you did not understand or care."
- "You faithfully instructed with My wisdom when your children were unteachable or forgetful."
- "You consistently and fairly disciplined even when your strong-willed children kept resisting month after month and year after year."
- "You repeatedly encouraged their talents and gifts even when they lacked confidence and wanted to give up in the face of setbacks."
- "You daily supplicated before Me even when My Presence did not seem to show up in their lives as you hoped and they made decisions contrary to My purposes."
- "Well done, good and faithful parent!"

*This is about you, not your kids! "God will reward each one according to the work each has done"* (1 Corinthians 3:8 GNT).

This is the legacy God intends for you to leave. This is about who you were, not who your children became, as important as that is. As we have said, we can only control our actions and reactions, not the outcomes in our kids.

This is all about *you*, not your children. Has God enlightened you on this? The greatest legacy you can leave your kids is who you were as a Christ-follower. What your children do with who you were is their choice.

Thus, we keep our end in mind. We realize that as we parent our children, God is parenting us. Here is how that would look in the form of the acronym G-U-I-D-E-S, during the parenting process in particular and in life generally:

**G**: Do I display a grateful heart toward what God gives to me?

**U**: Can I deal with anger and loss of heart because I believe and feel that God understands my concerns?

**I**: Am I always open to God's instruction, in every kind of setting and situation?

**D**: Do I accept God's loving discipline, never complaining that God is mean and unfair?

**E**: Have I used my talents for God's glory because I feel He encourages me to step out in faith?

**S**: Do I believe that Jesus and the Holy Spirit are making intercession for me, causing all things to work together for good?

If my basic answer to these questions is yes, then I understand that this is about Jesus and me.

Sarah experienced this in a challenging way when she battled breast cancer. She wrote in her journal:

As I faced my cancer diagnosis, I realized this was a chance of a lifetime. Would my life reflect Christ during this time of suffering? I claimed to know Him. Would my countenance and my words cause someone to desire Him? Would I praise and thank God regardless of the outcome? I felt as if God was saying that He wanted those looking on to see His power, His unfailing love, and His faithfulness.

Today Sarah is cancer free and continues to work and witness in all our lives. Her story is everyone's story. At one level or other this is all about me—all about my doing what God calls me to be and do no matter the people around me, including my kids.

This is the true legacy, the one we look back at from heaven with the Lord of lords and King of kings.

After Jonathan and I had talked at length one day about "parenting unto Christ," he sent a C. T. Studd (1860–1931) poem to me that fits perfectly with the concept of legacy:

## Only One Life[1]

> Two little lines I heard one day,
> Traveling along life's busy way;
> Bringing conviction to my heart,
> And from my mind would not depart;
> Only one life, 'twill soon be past,
> Only what's done for Christ will last.
>
> Only one life, a few brief years,
> Each with its burdens, hopes, and fears;
> Each with its days I must fulfill,
> Living for self or in His will;
> Only one life, 'twill soon be past,
> Only what's done for Christ will last.
>
> Give me, Father, a purpose deep,
> In joy or sorrow Thy word to keep;
> Faithful and true what e'er the strife,
> Pleasing Thee in my daily life;

*Only one life, 'twill soon be past,*
*Only what's done for Christ will last.*

*Only one life, yes only one,*
*Now let me say, "Thy will be done";*
*And when at last I'll hear the call,*
*I know I'll say "'twas worth it all";*
*Only one life, 'twill soon be past,*
*Only what's done for Christ will last!*

Begin again with the end in mind. Only parenting done as unto Christ will last. Truly, this is all about you and the legacy you leave your family.

## Love & Respect in the Family Conferences

For information about hosting a Love & Respect in the Family conference, go to www.loveandrespect.com /familyconference.

# Appendix A

# Love & Respect Goals
# for Our Family

To teach love and respect to your children, print or type the five principles listed below and post them in a prominent place or places in your home. The suggested things to say to younger or older children are only that: suggestions. Adapt them or develop your own comments according to the specific ages and needs of your children.

## Love & Respect Goals for Our Family

- We treat each other respectfully, even if someone does something that is not respectable.
- When we are treated unfairly or disrespectfully, we should say so in a respectful way.
- Children should obey, honor, and respect their parents.
- Parents always love their children, even when they are disrespectful.
- "We want to be a Love & Respect family."

**We treat each other respectfully, even if someone does something that is not respectable.**

With younger children say, "God says we are to love one another, and He also wants us to respect one another. Even when your brother does something mean, try to love him and respect him."

With older children say, "It is easy to respect others when they are doing everything that we like, but what if they are mean or unfair? God still wants us to love and respect them unconditionally. That means they don't have to earn our respect; we give it anyway even though they don't deserve it."

**When we are treated unfairly or disrespectfully, we should say so in a respectful way.**

With younger children get at eye level and say quietly, "When you are feeling frustrated by your sister, you need to come to me and use your respectful words about how you feel. I will help you. Do you understand?"

Or with the older child: "Calling your sister 'stupid' is obviously disrespectful. Mom and Dad don't talk that way, and we are sure you don't really want to talk that way either. Do you agree?"

**Children should obey, honor, and respect their parents.**

With younger children get at eye level and say, "The Bible says, 'Children, obey your parents in the Lord, for this is right. HONOR YOUR FATHER AND MOTHER' [Ephesians 6:1–2]. When something makes you angry, you will be tempted to be rude and not listen to us. God is asking you to obey us even when you think we don't understand or are being unfair. We will always try to understand and be fair. We have your best interests in mind."

Or with older children: "When God's Word says, 'Children,

obey your parents . . . honor your father and mother," it does not mean you are just a slave with no rights. God calls parents to be loving and fair, and sometimes it is hard to know exactly who or what is right. For example, we always need your brother's side of the story as well as yours, and we won't stop reminding you of what Jesus wants us all to do, like, 'Love one another.'"

When you believe your child can understand, talk about how obeying and honoring parents is the first commandment with a promise: "that it may go well with you and that you may enjoy long life on the earth" (Ephesians 6:3 NIV). Say something such as, "It is really very simple: when you obey us, it shows you respect us. When you do, things usually go very well for you. When you are disobedient or do things behind our backs, things won't go very well, and we have to discipline you. Which do you like better?"

**Parents always love their children, even when they are disrespectful.**

With younger children say, "God also has a command for Mommy and Daddy to always love you no matter what. We will always love you; there is nothing you can do to make us stop loving you. But that does not mean we are always happy with you and you are not always happy with us. We get angry sometimes, just as you do. But that does not mean we should stay angry or say rude things. If we do, we must apologize and so must you. No matter what happens, we want you to remember we love you with all our hearts."

With older children emphasize that while you love them, that does not mean everything goes just the way they want, nor do they get everything they want. Say something such as, "Mom and Dad must decide what is best, and that is a tough job. Sometimes we have to say no because we believe that is the most loving thing we can do for you. When you feel sad or sorry for yourself, remember we are your parents, and we are always here for you. We are not perfect, but we care. You mean everything to us."

**"We want to be a Love & Respect family."**

With younger children say, "Our love and respect for each other matters to God even more than it matters to us. When we love you and you respect and obey us, God is happy, and so are we."

With older children say, "No matter how hard it might be at times, we are committed to being firm and consistent with these wonderful truths, and we hope you will help us. We think this is very important because it is how Jesus wants us to treat each other. When we look at you or talk to you, it is as though we can imagine seeing Jesus just over your shoulder. As we love you, we are loving Jesus. It is the same with you. When you try to show us respect, imagine you can see Jesus just over our shoulders. When you respect us, you are respecting and loving Him. Remember, when you obey us, you are pleasing Jesus. The Bible says: 'Children, be obedient to your parents in all things, for this is well-pleasing to the Lord' [Colossians 3:20].

"Yes, there are times when we will fail to love you perfectly, and you will fail to respect us perfectly, but Jesus wants us to just get back up and try again. He forgives us, and we must forgive each other."

# Appendix B

# Checklists for Practicing Love & Respect in Your Parenting

**When It Comes to the Three Cycles**

1. When I get on the Family Crazy Cycle . . .
    a. will I blame my child for wrongly feeling unloved and for reacting with disrespect? or
    b. will I focus on my part of the Family Crazy Cycle and cease feeling disrespected and start reacting in more loving ways?
2. When it comes to the Family Energizing Cycle . . .
    a. will I demand that my child be respectful in order to motivate me to be loving? or
    b. will I demand of myself to be loving to influence my child's respectful responses?
3. When it comes to the Family Rewarded Cycle . . .
    a. will I expect my child to show me respect as to the Lord? or
    b. will I focus on me showing love toward my child as to the Lord?

**When Things Get a Bit Crazy**

1. Does my child appear disrespectful because I said or did something earlier that felt unloving to my child?
2. Do I need to reassure my child of my love and not take offense in the face of what feels disrespectful?

**Is My Child Reacting Negatively in Ways That Feel Disrespectful Because My Child . . .**

1. has unmet physical needs, and I need to Give to meet those needs?
2. has unmet emotional needs, and I need to Understand and empathize?
3. feels ignorant, and I need to Instruct my child?
4. has a lack of self-control, and I need to Discipline my child to help him become self-disciplined?
5. has fears facing the outside world, and I need to Encourage my child?
6. is under spiritual attack, and I need to Supplicate/pray for my child?

**Am I Balanced in Loving My Child?**

1. As for Giving to meet a child's needs and wants . . .
   a. do we give too little, showing a pattern of neglecting needs?
   b. do we give too much, showing a pattern of indulging wants?
2. As for Understanding so that we do not provoke or exasperate . . .
   a. do we understand too little, being without empathy and expecting too much?

b. do we understand too much, psychoanalyzing and feeding self-pity?

3. As for **I**nstructing so that a child can know and apply God's wisdom . . .

a. do we instruct too little, withholding God's truth that would help and guide them?

b. do we instruct too much, overly preaching and moralizing, which turns them off?

4. As for **D**isciplining so that a child can learn to correct hurtful choices . . .

a. do we discipline too little, showing a pattern of permissiveness?

b. do we discipline too much, showing a pattern of authoritarianism?

5. As for **E**ncouraging so that a child can develop God-given gifts in the world . . .

a. do we encourage too little, being pessimistic, critical, and judgmental?

b. do we encourage too much, being superficial, unrealistic, and false?

6. As for **S**upplicating so that a child can experience God's touch and truth . . .

a. do we pray too little, not asking God to work in our children?

b. do we pray too much, substituting courageous parenting with prayer?

## Am I Depending on God to Do What I Cannot?

1. When I **G**ive, do I pray that God helps my child (and me) have a *thankful and grateful heart*?

2. When I **U**nderstand, do I pray that God helps my child (and me) have a *calm and tranquil heart*?

3. When I **I**nstruct, do I pray that God helps my child (and me) have a *teachable spirit*?

4. When I **D**iscipline, do I pray that God helps my child (and me) *have true remorse*?

5. When I **E**ncourage, do I pray that God helps my child (and me) *have courage*?

6. When I **S**upplicate, do I pray that God helps my child (and me) have a *trusting and obedient heart*?

# NOTES

## Part One: The Family Crazy Cycle

1. The apostles referred to believers as "beloved children" (1 Corinthians 4:14; Ephesians 5:1; 1 John 3:2). The Greek word for "beloved" is *agapetos*. God loved His children, setting His affection upon them. But not only does the metaphor of "beloved children" apply to the people of God, but the metaphor springs from the reality of agape—an unconditional love—parents have for their children. Children are the object of parental affection. They are beloved. The child does not earn such love. *Agapetos* is a birthright. Such *agapetos* is observed between mother and nursing baby, to which Paul refers in 1 Thessalonians 2:7–8. Children need this love, and God designed parents to give it.

## Chapter 2: Stopping the Family Crazy Cycle, Part I: Decode

1. In Colossians 3:21, the Greek text speaks of exasperating or embittering the child. The NIV, for example, renders the verse: "Fathers, do not embitter your children, or they will become discouraged." I prefer the NASB translation, which renders the verse: "Fathers, do not exasperate [or 'aggravate' (NLT)] your children, so that they will not lose heart." In my observations, discouraged children who have lost heart are usually more exasperated than embittered, although some embittered children eventually give up in defeat.

2. Some commentaries imply that Colossians 3:21 and Ephesians

255

6:4 are cross-reference passages that mean essentially the same thing. However, Colossians 3:21 uses two Greek words not found in Ephesians 6:4, and Ephesians 6:4 uses a Greek word not found in Colossians 3:21. In Colossians 3:21, Paul used the word *athumeo*, which means "to be disheartened or to lose heart." In other words, parents can cause their children to become discouraged, to give up, or to lose hope. Ephesians 6:4 says nothing about loss of heart in the child. Furthermore, Paul used the Greek word *parorgizo* in Ephesians 6:4, but not in Colossians 3:21, and he used the Greek word *erethizo* in Colossians 3:21, but not in Ephesians 6:4. *Parorgizo* is a compound word that essentially means "to provoke to anger," whereas *erethizo* comes from *eretho*, which can mean "to stir up to anger," but also conveys more simply the idea of "stirred, to stir up, or exasperate." When comparing *parorgizo* and *erethizo*, is this a distinction without a difference? If there is no difference, we can say, as many do, that the two passages mean the same thing: children can be provoked or exasperated to the point of anger, which usually pushes them to the point of discouragement and loss of heart. We would then say that Colossians 3:21 enlarges the idea in Ephesians 6:4, which implies discouragement. On the other hand, Paul could be describing two types of children: the angry/embittered child (Ephesians 6:4) and the discouraged/defeated child (Colossians 3:21). Psychologically, then, we would be dealing with an angry child with clenched fists or with a discouraged child with drooped shoulders. The first child explodes in anger whereas the second deflates in defeat. The unfair parent ignites righteous indignation in the first child, who angrily screams, "You cannot treat me this way!" whereas the unfair parent sets a standard that the second child cannot reach, and the child collapses in defeat, mumbling, "I can't do it . . . I can't do it." At the extreme level, one kicks the wall in an act of rage and almost seems homicidal; the other falls on the floor crying and almost seems suicidal. So where does this leave us? Ephesians 6:4 stresses that a father must not provoke his child to the point where he erupts in anger. Colossians 3:21 stresses that a father must not exasperate his child to the point where he deflates and loses heart.

## Chapter 3: Stopping the Family Crazy Cycle, Part II: Defuse

1. For forty years I collected stories from people. This is one of those stories. In this instance I did a series on fathering and asked the congregation to send me stories. I numbered these stories but removed the name to protect the innocent. However, either I lost the list of names, or I stored it away in a storage unit to be found years later. Regardless, this story had the number 72 assigned to it but without a name. Therefore, I apologize to this dad for not contacting him. If you read this and are the dad, please let me know. If you are the source, please forgive me and allow me to correct my mistake. In wrath, remember mercy.

## Chapter 4: Give: Not Too Little, Not Too Much

1. To get the complete story on how Jacob's favoritism toward Joseph caused much family strife and heartache, read Genesis 37–50. God protected Joseph after he was sold into slavery, and eventually he reconciled with his brothers.

## Chapter 5: Understand: Put Yourself in Their Shoes

1. For example, Rebekah, Isaac's wife, loved her son Jacob more than his twin brother, Esau, and her favoritism and deception on Jacob's part caused much turmoil in the family. Esau got so frustrated he would have killed Jacob if he had not fled and stayed away for many years. For the full story, see Genesis 25:19–33:20.

2. Note that I quote the New International Version of Hebrews 4:15, which uses the word "empathize" for the Greek word *sumpatheo*. Many translations of Hebrews 4:15 state: "For we do not have a high priest who is unable to *sympathize* with our weaknesses." This can be misleading to many people today because they define "sympathy" as feeling sorry for someone even when you cannot fully identify with their experience or pain. By using "empathize" the translators of the NIV come much closer to describing the feelings our Lord has toward us. The Greek word *sumpatheo* means "to have a fellow feeling with, commiserate, have compassion for." It is used in different ways in Scripture, but often the idea of empathy—understanding and

sharing another's feelings or thoughts—is being conveyed, as it is here in Hebrews 4:15. See also the New Living Translation: "This High Priest of ours understands our weaknesses . . ." and Eugene Peterson's vivid paraphrase, *The Message*: "We don't have a priest who is out of touch with our reality. He's been through weakness and testing, experienced it all—all but the sin."

## Chapter 6: Instruct: Not Too Much . . . but Just Enough "Stuff Like That"

1. Obviously our main goal should be having our children come to faith in Christ, but sadly this is not always the case. The Barna Research Group surveyed a group of Christian parents and found that the number-one thing they wanted for their children was not salvation, but a "good education." A relationship with Christ was third on the list. See "Parents Describe How They Raise Their Children," February 28, 2005. http://www .barna.org/barna-update/article/5-barna-update/184-parents -describe-how-they-raise-their-children?q=salvation+children +good+education+parents.

2. "Money for the Preacher," http://www.christian-jokes.org/jokes95 .html, author unknown.

3. This has been widely reprinted and attributed to Twain, but has never been found in his works, though various Twain groups and the Twain Papers staff have searched for it. See more at: http:// quotationsbook.com/quote/45037/#sthash.vHB55bHK.dpuf.

4. For an informative and revealing article on how the brain of the typical adolescent develops, see "Adolescent angst: 5 facts about the teen brain," http://www.foxnews.com/health/2012/07/09 /adolescent-angst-5-facts-about-teen-brain/. As teenagers grow older, the limbic system (emotional seat of the brain) comes under greater control of the prefrontal cortex, an area just behind the forehead, associated with planning, impulse control, and higher-order thought.

## Chapter 7: Discipline: Confront . . . Correct . . . Comfort

1. Many ideas for making and using reward charts for obeying

family rules are available on the Internet. You are sure to find something that will fit your children's ages and stages. Just Google "Reward charts for children."

2. Parental teamwork is critical in rearing your children. See chapter 10, "Teamwork."

## Chapter 8: Encourage: Equip Them to Succeed and Not Lose Heart

1. See Nick Charles, CNN/SI, "By George: Brett Honored the Game with Respect," http://sportsillustrated.cnn.com/baseball /mlb/news/1999/07/22/pageone_brett.
2. Margie M. Lewis and Gregg Lewis, *The Hurting Parent* (Grand Rapids: Zondervan, 2009), 100.
3. Source unknown. I have used this story often in sermons over the years.
4. Dr. Ross Campbell, *How to Really Love Your Child* (Colorado Springs, CO: David C. Cook, 2010), 75.

## Chapter 9: Supplicate: Pray . . . with Confidence That God Listens to Us and Speaks to Them

1. Note, too, that after Paul instructed children and parents in Ephesians 6:1–4, he urged believers to be "praying always with all prayer and supplication in the Spirit" (Ephesians 6:18 NKJV). In all of life, and in parenting particularly, we need to look to God in supplication.
2. I did my graduate school research at Michigan State University as part of a PhD dissertation: "A Descriptive Analysis of Strong Evangelical Fathers." A major purpose of the inquiry was to investigate the fathering style of preselected strong fathers as perceived by the strong father himself, his wife, and his adult child. Study was made of the strong father's involvement, consistency, awareness, and nurture with his children. Areas studied included time commitment to children, involvement in discipline, involvement in education, marital interaction, dealing with crisis, showing affection, modeling, financial provision, spiritual development, allowing freedom of expression,

and knowing one's child. The profile that emerged from the study showed strong fathers to be developmentally aware of their children, consistent in dealing with and relating to their children, attentive and caring listeners, good models of maturity, able to deal with crisis knowledgeably and positively, and able to provide financially.

3. Seeking permission to quote her, I contacted her eight years after she e-mailed me. She commented, "As an update, he is now eighteen, is heading to college to study music (we serve a mighty God!), and has continued to grow in his relationship with Jesus. He has such a gift for pointing us to Him just when we need it. Thank you for your ministry. It has had a profound impact on how I raised both of my sons."

4. When Mueller began building these orphanages he had two shillings (fifty cents) in his pocket. When he died in 1898 there were five immense buildings made of solid granite, housing two thousand orphans, who never missed a meal because the Lord always provided. See J. Gilchrist Lawson, *Deeper Experiences of Famous Christians* (Anderson, IN: Warner Press, 1911).

## Chapter 10: Teamwork: How to Put Your Children First

1. Divorce is biblically justified for habitual adultery and permanent desertion (Matthew 19:9; 1 Corinthians 7:15), but it is absolutely a last resort. Love and Respect Ministries was founded on, and is dedicated to, the mission of helping husbands and wives save their marriages by meeting each other's most basic needs: hers for love, his for respect.

2. Note that Ephesians 5:33, the flagship verse of the Love & Respect Connection, states that the husband "must love his wife as he loves himself, and the wife must respect her husband" (NIV). Then a few verses later Paul goes on to give God's command to fathers (and by implication mothers as well): "Do not exasperate your children; instead, bring them up in the training and instruction of the Lord" (Ephesians 6:4 NIV). I do not think it was accidental that Paul dealt first with marriage, then with parenting as he laid down principles for Christian living.

3. We are not saved by good works. Salvation is available through

God's grace, His free gift to those who believe (Ephesians 2:8–9). Once we are saved we can do good works to glorify God, but we are still capable of slipping back into sinful behavior, which we all do.

4. Professional survey data published in Shaunti Feldhahn, *For Women Only: What You Need to Know About the Inner Lives of Men* (Sisters, OR: Multnomah, 2004). Survey performed for Shaunti Feldhahn by Decision Analyst and tabulated by Analytic Focus.

5. Unconditional love for the wife and unconditional respect for the husband are two vital needs. Many women have difficulty with respecting men who have not "earned" their respect. Unconditional means just that. A man does not earn his wife's unconditional respect, just as a wife does not have to earn her husband's love. Both are given freely in obedience and devotion to God. For more on unconditional love or respect, go to www.loveandrespect.com/unconditional love.

6. See "Conclusion: Pink and Blue Can Make God's Purple," Emerson Eggerichs, *Love & Respect* (Nashville: Thomas Nelson, 2004), 297ff.

## Chapter 11: Parenting Pink and Blue

1. "Out of the thirty thousand genes in the human genome, the less than one percent variation between the sexes is small. But that percentage difference influences every single cell in our bodies—from the nerves that register pleasure and pain to the neurons that transmit perception, thoughts, feelings, and emotions."—Louann Brizendine, *The Female Brain* (New York: Broadway Books, 2006), 2.

2. "Males and females become reactive to different kinds of stress. Girls begin to react more to relationship stresses and boys to challenges to their authority. Relationship conflict is what drives a teen girl's stress system wild. She needs to be liked and socially connected; a teen boy needs to be respected" (Ibid., 34–35).

3. Shaunti Feldhahn, *For Parents Only* (Sisters, OR: Multnomah, 2007), 136.

4. Brizendine, *The Female Brain*, 24, 29.

5. Ibid., 8.
6. Ibid., 15–18.
7. Understanding pink and blue differences is important, but what about the differences between blue and blue and pink and pink? Fathers and sons have their own language and communication challenges, as do mothers and daughters.

## Chapter 13: Because He Loves Us, No Matter What . . . We Love Them . . . No Matter What

1. Since Psalm 127 was written by King Solomon, he was apparently referring to the nation of Israel and the temple he built at God's request (1 Kings 5:1–6:14). Another meaning for the word *house* in Hebrew is "a household or a family." Many commentators believe a strong secondary meaning of *house* in this psalm has to be the family because children are spotlighted in verses 3–5. For other verses where the Hebrew word *bah'-yith* refers to a person's family, see 1 Chronicles 13:14; 2 Chronicles 21:13; Zechariah 12:12.

2. As I teach in conferences all over the country I continually interact with people, often mothers, who tell me if their son "doesn't deserve respect I shouldn't have to give him respect . . . this only lets him off the hook and demands that I give up my parental authority." My answer is: "Absolutely not! We are talking about respectfully confronting and disciplining the wrongdoing with the full weight of our authority—boy or girl. The unconditional gift we give our tot or teen is a respectful attitude when correcting the disobedience." Parents who understand how Christ unconditionally loves and honors them but still disciplines them as necessary can learn to lovingly and respectfully confront their children and discipline them. But to continue to show a child—especially a son—that he must earn our respectful attitude is to justify our contempt and to lose his heart. This is not about a tot or teen earning our honorable demeanor but about our being honorable regardless of their demeanor. This is about what we display, not what they deserve. Thus, we read in Scripture the spiritual law that we are to display a respectful attitude toward undeserving people. "Always show respect . . . not only to those

who are kind and thoughtful, but also to those who are cruel" (1 Peter 2:18 CEV). Most see the unconditional love in the Bible (Matthew 5:46) but overlook the teaching on unconditional respect (Romans 12:10; 1 Peter 2:17). (See chapter 7 and the four steps in "Discipline," page 98.)

## Chapter 14: Beware of the "Outcomes Trap"

1. Some of the most significant research done on children as moral and spiritual beings is that of Dr. Robert Coles of Harvard, who spent thirty years studying the moral life of children. According to Scott London, Coles, author of *The Moral Life of Children* (New York: Atlantic Monthly Press, 1986), "feels that no one in his field of child psychiatry, or in related fields, has fully appreciated the ability of even relatively young children to pose questions about the meaning and 'moral significance' of life." See www.scottlondon.com/articles/coles.html.

2. My father later came to Christ my freshman year at Wheaton College. The Lord loved and forgave my dad, as did my mom, my sister, and I. My dad changed. He stopped those sins of earlier years. He died knowing he would be with Christ. In fact, before the surgery that proved unsuccessful and took his life, I asked Dad, "If the surgery is not successful, are you ready to die?" He nodded yes. Dad knew the Lord and had His peace. He was forgiven.

3. The prophet Jeremiah placed Samuel alongside Moses in stature (Jeremiah 15:1); nonetheless, his boys opted for greed as their creed.

## Conclusion: What Kind of Legacy Will You Leave?

1. Concerning the poem "Only One Life," Andrew L Bowker, with WEC Publications, which is part of WEC International, which C. T. Studd founded, commented, "We believe the poem you quote to be by C. T. Studd, but it does not occur in *Quaint Rhymes of a Quondam Cricketer*, which is a collection of such pieces, and we have not been able to trace it to any other source. C. T. Studd wrote a large quantity of material and produced many tracts and booklets as he challenged particularly the Christian young men of his day to sacrifice everything for Jesus. It may have been in one of those . . ."

# About the Author

**D**r. Emerson Eggerichs is an internationally known expert on male-female relationships. The author of several books, including the national bestseller *Love & Respect*, which has sold more than 1.5 million copies, Emerson and his wife, Sarah, present the Love & Respect conference both live and by video to thousands of people each year. They have been honored to speak to groups such as the NFL, the PGA, members of Congress, and the United States military.

Prior to launching their ministry, Dr. Eggerichs was the senior pastor of Trinity Church in Lansing, Michigan, for nineteen years. He has graduate degrees from Wheaton College and Dubuque Seminary and a PhD in child and family ecology from Michigan State University. Married since 1973, Emerson and Sarah live in Grand Rapids, Michigan, and have three adult children. He is the founder and president of Love and Respect Ministries.

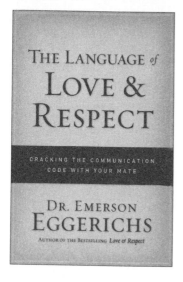

THE LANGUAGE of LOVE & RESPECT

CRACKING THE COMMUNICATION CODE WITH YOUR MATE

DR. EMERSON EGGERICHS

AUTHOR OF THE BESTSELLING Love & Respect

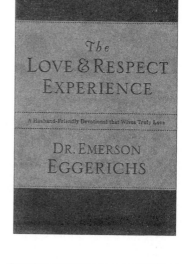

The LOVE & RESPECT EXPERIENCE

A Husband-Friendly Devotional that Wives Truly Love

DR. EMERSON EGGERICHS

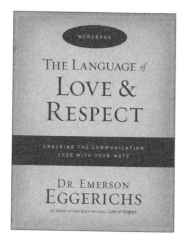

WORKBOOK

THE LANGUAGE of LOVE & RESPECT

CRACKING THE COMMUNICATION CODE WITH YOUR MATE

DR. EMERSON EGGERICHS

AUTHOR OF THE BEST-SELLING Love & Respect

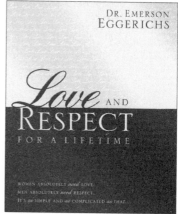

DR. EMERSON EGGERICHS

Love AND RESPECT FOR A LIFETIME

WOMEN ABSOLUTELY need LOVE.
MEN ABSOLUTELY need RESPECT.
IT'S as SIMPLE and as COMPLICATED as THAT...